TRANSITIONS

Finding Hope in Change

❧

Chris Ann Waters

Transitions

Finding Hope in Change

CHRIS ANN WATERS

TRANSITIONS
Copyright © 2020 Chris Ann Waters

ISBN 978-1-938796-77-7
Library of Congress Control Number: 2020922451
Self-Help • Death, Grief, Bereavement • Transitional Moments

Published by Fruitbearer Publishing, LLC
P. O. Box 777, Georgetown, DE 19947
302.856.6649 • FAX 302.856.7742
www.fruitbearer.com • info@fruitbearer.com

Photographs by Chris Ann Waters
Graphic Design by Candy Abbott

Scripture quotations are taken from The Holy Bible,
King James Version. Public domain.

Printed and bound in the United States of America

Dedication

To
Bea and Cecil Withers

Your faith in Jesus, love, encouragement, and generosity of spirit help keep my faith and love vibrant. I carry deep love and thanksgiving for you and the ocean of memories we made; memories of inestimable worth that live on.

To God be the glory for His perfect promises for all that is to be in this life until we are reunited in the life everlasting through belief in Jesus Christ. Indeed there is a time for every season, and a time for every purpose under Heaven (Ecclesiastes 3:1). The Lord has been exceedingly generous to let us live out our seasons and purposes together. He brought you Home first, but there is no distance between us in the Spirit. For now, I occupy here with an intent to love and live as you exemplified. Until that redemptive transition is known to me, I look up to where He and you are, confident of our reunion and eternity we shall share together.

Mark the perfect man, and behold the upright,
for the end of that man is peace.

Psalm 37:37

To everything there is a season,
and a time to every purpose under Heaven.

A time to be born, and time to die;
a time to plant, and a time to pluck up that which is planted;

A time to kill, and a time to heal;
a time to break down, and a time to build up;

A time to weep, and a time to laugh;
a time to mourn, and a time to dance;

A time to cast away stones, and a time to gather stones together;
a time to embrace, and a time to refrain from embracing;

A time to get, and a time to lose;
a time to keep, and a time to cast away;

A time to rend, and a time to sew;
a time to keep silence, and a time to speak;

A time to love, and a time to hate;
a time of war, and a time of peace.

Ecclesiastes 3:1-8

Acknowledgements

There are different people to acknowledge for their prayers, support, and encouragement. This is by no means comprehensive but a brief summary. Others I shall communicate with via personal pen and letters.

Always and forever, God, Jesus and Holy Spirit, You are my all in all. Every breath and step belongs to You. For everything You are, have done, and do, my praise, thanksgiving, and allegiance. Thank You, Lord, for the gifts of writing and photography that are blessings that have filled the years so beautifully. I pray these gifts make a difference for souls spent with You.

To my publisher, Candy Abbott and all at Fruitbearer, my ongoing thanksgiving for your skill, creativity, patience, and wisdom given to this project, and for the generosity of self you give to our friendship. How generous is our Lord.

To family members and friends who are on this journey with me. You know who you are and what our relationships mean. Somehow and somewhere down the road of years what you have given of yourself has brought me to where I am. For this I am thankful. I pray that I have made a beneficent difference in your life. I pray that my witness is worthy and memorable. This be so, I could not ask to have done more for you with my life. God bless and sustain you throughout this life and in the Eternal Life. Be there. It would not be Heaven without you.

To my fellow prayer warriors everywhere. Day by day and decade by decade we continue to advance God's Kingdom via God's Word and the fortifying act of prayer. For all we do collectively, and for all you do for me personally, I remain invigorated, steady, and prepared. My cup runneth over.

Through it all, through it all,
I've learned to trust in Jesus,
I've learned to trust in God.

Through it all, through it all,
I've learned to depend upon His Word.

— Andrae' Crouch

Table of Contents

Introduction xi

1. Missed Calls 1

2. On the Brink... 4

3. Fathers and Days 7

4. Touched 10

5. God's Math and the Economy 13

6. Off Key.. 16

7. A Little Bit Longer... 19

8. Space.. 22

9. Empty Nests.. 25

10. Spineless.. 28

11. Forgiveness and a Shih Tzu 31

12. Until Death Do Us Part 34

13. The Piers of Our Lives 36

14. A Parent's Loss 39

15. Taking Advantage of the Slope 42

16. Linked by Love 45

17. Final Hugs and Finish Lines 48

18. Later.. 51

19. The Glistening Christ.. 54

20. Spiderman, Sandals, and Yesterdays 57

21. So I Did 60

22. Gratitude 63

23. V8 or Ginger Ale 67

24. Blind Faith 69

25. The Price of Memories 72

26. Yet 75

27. What If You Had Not Given of Yourself 78

28. Replacements 81

29. Thoughts on Pet Loss 84

30. Time 87

31. A Matter of Respect 89

32. The Strategic Holy Spirit 92

33. Notions 95

34. Tables of Grace 98

35. Who Me? 100

36. Finish This 103

37. Conclusion 106

About the Author 110

Order Information 111

Introduction

Our days and years involve simple and complex transitions which have the potential to direct us to fulfill our purposes. Because life's fluidity brings constant movement, changes in our lives serve as a catalyst to prompt us to become what we are meant to become. Changes in our lives—anticipated or unbidden—may or may not at first glance appear to produce circumstances that have any meaningful purpose. But all transitions in our lives hold enormous potential to shape our character and life's course. Ultimately the transitions we meet and live through are indeed purposeful, whether purposes are revealed or concealed. Only time and the development of our will makes known what transitions will produce.

Transitions is a collection of vignettes that describe different kinds of life experiences we encounter. These chapters sketch different challenges and changes that produce loss and grief of some sort and measure. Hope is the thread of similarity woven into each. Hope is present when God is present. The accompaniment of God throughout transitions infuses every situation with hope, even when hope is unclear and unfelt. This anthology offers experiences familiar to some degree. While the kind of transitions and losses highlighted in each chapter differ, the quotient of hope available is always the same—steady and limitless. Hope is what God gives, hope that God's promise of a purposeful outcome will be trusted even if it is not yet revealed.

There are questions about our lives that may be unanswered. That is where faith comes in. Faith in God is a decision to trust the God who knows best about us and our circumstances and is with us in all of life's transitions. God knows the answers to the whys in our lives. Each of us has faced or will face times in life overwhelming, convoluted and extreme in experience and emotion; so much so that reasonable thinking brings little or no clarity. These are times we can spend seeking logic and acceptance. However, the real acceptance is in turning such matters over to God. An act that can be a struggle. Yet, releasing matters to God brings a silent yet steady relinquishment of seeking human reason via human means. With such release comes opportunity for God to fill up space in the heart and mind that had been occupied with *why?* Squirming, trudging, walking, and resigning ourselves to individual life transitions, takes faith. Faith beyond ourselves. Faith beyond circumstances. Faith in God through Jesus Christ. With the strength of the Lord, going through transitions is possible.

To let go best is to hold tightly to God. Hold to His promises and His timing. Not ours. A grueling process at times. But the finest faith in the Lord is often developed and furthered because of loss and grief that require full reliance on the Lord for His strength, a reliance that can eventually reveal to a griever the reliability and strength of God. He is the Overseer of His creation. People are His highest creation. *Let us make man in our image, after our likeness* (Genesis 1:26). Finding purpose in certain transitions can be an arduous assignment. The Bible states *With open face beholding as in a glass the glory of the Lord, are changed into the same image from glory to glory* (2 Corinthians 3:18). Glory endowed to people is really the glorification of God, to whom all glory belongs.

Eternity shall reveal answers to questions that for now remain blessedly veiled. God has wisdom that is incomparable to ours. *For My thoughts are not your thoughts; neither are your ways My ways, saith the Lord* (Isaiah 55:8). God knows everything, which includes the reasons for life's changes. *He knows the end from the beginning* (Isaiah 46:10). Yielding to the wisdom of God is a lifelong activity. Yieldedness is not a one-time process that completes; it is an ongoing flow of faith blended with obedience intended to produce the benefits of acceptance, faith and peace.

For many years I have written *Transitions,* an anthology about Christian faith and encouragement necessary in times of grief. As a bereavement specialist and hospice provider of chaplaincy and spiritual care for 25 years, I had been asked for some time to put these writings into book form. This book contains stories and experiences, ones to which persons can generally relate. Trimming down the content was the greatest challenge as I had not realized how prolific the years had been. One morning while walking, the Lord gave me the inspiration to incorporate my photography into this book. Thus, all the photographs are from my personal collection taken during decades of travel and seasons of living. Photography has been a tremendous blessing to me throughout my life. I trust the Lord to share these photographs here and use this visual inspiration as only He can for purposes He alone can see.

This book is written by a Christian lady living in America. I believe in the Bible, its truth and inestimable worth. Jesus is my Saviour. The only One who can save one from sin and Hell because of His loving sacrifice on Calvary's Cross. From that perspective, my writings are penned. For those who share my belief in Jesus as Saviour, this book will serve as encouragement and reinforcement. For those who do not yet believe in Jesus as Saviour, it is my prayer that you will come to believe. Transitions in life are individual yet universal. As distinctive as transitions and purposes are in each life, Jesus is distinctive in His way of connecting with each person. He knows how to touch a heart and break through the questions, fears, pains, and doubts to establish a relationship with Him. The slight nudges received that seem *out of character* may be the very catalyst God uses to draw persons near to Him. Quite often, God uses times of pain and vulnerability— times of need—to establish relationships with people.

As this book goes to press, COVID-19 is in the world. It has shifted the lives of everyone as the infrastructure of life has been altered for a season. People seek stability as this unprecedented event has had innumerable ramifications on all segments of society. The transitions people are making due to grief and/or stark changes in daily life make means of coping essential. It is my prayer that this book serves our times.

How? Why? Why now? These questions continue. They will until the Lord returns for His people collectively or we return to Him one by one. Because God is all-knowing and all-loving, the answers to our questions have the potential to dissolve into faith. Faith pleases God. *Without faith it is impossible to please him* (Hebrews 11:6). It is my prayer that this book will provide you with a governing awareness of His presence, a measure of solace, encouragement, and a silken strand of hope that enables you to carry on and believe in purposes beyond circumstances. God intends for our lives to have meaning and produce rich and rewarding earthly and Eternal legacies. Going through life's transitions and letting God make them purposeful is, in large part, the making of our legacies. Thank you for giving your time and attention to this book. God bless you. May you bless God. May His heart and hand keep you throughout this life and Eternally.

Chris Ann Waters

Chapter 1

Missed Calls

But know that the Lord hath set apart him that is godly for himself;
the Lord will hear when I call unto Him.

Psalm 4:3

During the off season, a group of loved ones and I went on a tour of what would soon become the old Yankee Stadium. The youngsters in our group could not wait to get there. For me (and the other adults) these young people's reactions were as interesting to observe as the highlights of the stadium. The boys were captivated by the locker room, press box, Monument Park, and especially the telephone in the dugout.

While all features of the park were interesting, for the young people, there was a mystique to the telephone. They wanted to sit beside it and get their pictures taken, individually and as a group. It was fascinating for them to see the physical point of contact that made for changes on the field, primarily the pitchers that would come to the mound. The adults in our group found it comical to watch the youngsters role-play as though they were calling the shots! Captivated by the intrigue I witnessed in these young ones over the phone, I wondered if they would grow into the confidence that, as Christians, communication with God is faster and more profound than the kind that impresses them now.

Contact with God is continuously available. His heart is always open to listen. Anyone, at any time, can call on God to share a happy thought, release a burden, ask for guidance, and call on Him in silence due to life's pains or to say, *I love You.* He hears. He answers. Nothing pleases God more than to be a part of the lives of those He created. He watches from a distance the details of each experience, and welcomes the communication that keeps Him part of our daily routines and extraordinary events.

God knows that life challenges come along that can be so overwhelming they prevent one from reaching out to Him. Such experiences can be emotionally difficult. He understands. Changes and challenges that can make one feel burdened include the death of a spouse, parent or friend. The death of a child can leave one speechless for years. A divorce, an illness, a matter too complex to discuss as well as a myriad of other transitions and strange life-places that make God seem distant and one too weak to pray, are realities for some. Loss of one's faith, voice, spirit and hope often come as a result of such pain. God sees. God understands. God can and will help.

Even though life's pains are challenging, they need not be faced alone. God is there. He wants to hear from us. At all times. He is waiting. We must initiate the call. Maybe all that one can muster is simply folded hands, kneeling quietly, or saying, "Jesus." Although small an effort and simple words, whatever is offered is enough for the Holy Spirit to carry the transmission. Trust that. The Holy Spirit is more powerful than is obvious. He is active in the unseen and unheard. He will fill in the gaps. But He needs the smallest seed of faith to initiate the call. Although seemingly weak, this little effort is a call placed to God. Without these starts, there are missed calls, missed opportunities to connect with God and enter into a time of fellowship with Him and receive strength throughout life's circumstances.

Leaving Yankee Stadium that day, I knew I would smile whenever I watched the Yankees play on television, especially if I caught a glimpse of the telephone in the dugout. I also knew it would be my continuous prayer that these boys would grow into men whose faith would absorb them rather than the world absorb their faith. I prayed God would not suffer from their absence because of missed calls to Him, calls God waits to answer.

Lord, throughout the familiar and surreal experiences of life, You are there. Thank You for Your presence in our lives even when pains are difficult to bear and calls to You are not made. Thank You for Your heart that listens. Holy Spirit, help us to be mindful to call upon You. When we do, You take our morsels of faith to grow our relationship with You and give us wisdom and strength to carry on. In Jesus' Name, Amen.

Chapter 2

On the Brink

He is despised and rejected of men;
a man of sorrows and acquainted with grief, and we hid as it were our faces from Him.
He was despised, and we esteemed Him not.
Surely He hath borne our griefs and carried our sorrows,
yet we did esteem Him stricken, smitten of God, and afflicted.

Isaiah 53:3

When I was in college I worked during the summers as a tour escort for a travel agency. My territory included the New England states and Niagara Falls. I studied much about these regions and then explained this to the tourists. When Nik Wallenda recently made a historic walk across Niagara Falls, I watched intently, never dreaming that a place so familiar to me would be the site of such a human feat. I prayed Nick would make it safely across as the waters rushed around him and beneath him. As he walked gingerly along the thin wire fastened between the American and Canadian borders, Nick spoke the names God and Jesus over and over again. He believed the Father, Son, and Holy Spirit were with him as he walked. He did indeed make it safely to the other side.

The use of drugs and alcohol in our culture have become so commonplace that their addictive properties and destructive powers are dismissed and/or disguised until one is walking a tightrope to make it from addiction to recovery. Drugs and alcohol can seem simple social and recreational means for relaxation and socialization. However, they have the potential to become strong habits, so strong that they ruin lives, marriages, careers, and hope for the future. When individuals use drugs and alcohol, he or she— regardless of age, gender, education or financial status—may not realize they are on the brink of developing an addiction and meeting with painful consequences that follow.

Drug and alcohol usage can cause grief. Deep grief. Reasons for losses that result in grief include drunk driving, homicides, suicides, date rape, job loss, marital strife, divorce, custody battles, academic decline, athletic decline, criminal offenses, and theft. In addition, there is loss of normal brain function, normal reflex skills, and cognitive ability. In conjunction with these losses are the emotional ramifications that are complex for the individual and those he or she loves. When one person losses self-control, others are at risk and loved ones suffer, too.

For those who have suffered physical, mental, emotional and spiritual pains due to drugs and alcohol, these experiences leave a mark. Whether the pain has been personal or related to watching a loved one self-destruct due to drugs and drinking, it is a sorrowful and difficult process. Jesus knows what it feels like to be in such a state. He can fully identify with human pain. He suffered the greatest of human, emotional, and spiritual pain. But love kept Him on the cross so that He could be the One to shed the blood that would cleanse sin and give a fresh start and new hope to people. His love is with each person. Whatever poor choices have been made, Jesus accepts. Jesus will never reject anyone who calls upon Him in faith.

To be on the brink of an addiction is to be on the verge of a job loss, a divorce, a car accident. But the subtlety of alcohol and drug usage can make one think *I can handle it* or

That would never happen to me, or to my husband, my son. Wrong. It can. It has. It does. The culture has normalized alcohol and drug usage through advertisements, sports, and in all kinds of social settings that its dangers are often concealed. Dangers become glaring when something painful, something tragic, occurs.

God intends for our time in this world to be rich and full of hope. He sent Jesus to us to be the reason why our hope can be full and unending. Using drugs and alcohol to cope with school problems, bullying, breakups with boyfriends or girlfriends, to escape from life's responsibilities, to cope with the stresses of work and family, or to avoid making decisions and taking responsibility for one's life, is neither beneficial nor honest. Recognizing that drugs and alcohol are being used for the wrong reasons and getting help is beneficial. For you. For those who love you. There is no shame in reaching out for help. Making one phone call or sending one email to admit a problem is an act of courage and honesty. That one act to reach out for help could prevent addiction and even save a life. Maybe yours.

When Nik Wallenda walked across that fine wire to make it to the other side, he continuously said aloud, "God" and "Jesus." They were with him. Anyone who calls out to God and Jesus is a voice that will be heard. Whatever fine wire you or someone you love is walking today, God and Jesus are listening with their hearts of love and arms of strength to hold you up and get you to the other side safely. Never let go.

Holy Spirit, touch those who read this so that Your inspiration for what is needed is received and acted upon. Help those who suffer the strains of bondage to drugs and alcohol. Help those who grieve because of what they have experienced and witnessed due to the destructive results of these substances. Thank You, Father God and Lord Jesus, for Your precious presence and open heart to hear and to help those who call to You and receive Your love that saves and soothes. In Jesus' Name forevermore, Amen.

Chapter 3

Fathers and Days

A word spoken in due season, how good it is.

Proverbs 15:23

Early June brings a host of personal remembrances and historic accounts of D-Day. When this anniversary is marked, it is moving to read or listen to elderly war veterans speak of their experience. This year I had the opportunity to listen to a veteran speak specifically about the brotherhood the men felt. He explained that the danger and the unknown created a bond between the men that was strong, unusual, and often lasting.

One point this gentleman made that was of particular interest was when he spoke about hidden wounds. He and other soldiers were inclined to conceal their wounds as best they could in order not to be taken out of combat. They wanted to stay with their fellow soldiers. Moreover, he explained that men were embarrassed to be wounded and taken out of combat. Therefore, they would hide injuries as best they could in order to continue participating in battle. This same desire was expressed by a soldier I once met at Walter Reed. The officer put it this way, *I want to heal and get back there. We have to be there for each other.*

Several years ago I was invited to Walter Reed Army Medical Center in Washington, D.C. to meet with wounded officers who had returned from Iraq and Afghanistan. I was moved for many reasons. However, the camaraderie among the officers was particularly impressive. A friend of mine arranged for my visit there as he had an affiliation with Walter Reed, and he felt my skills in bereavement and communication would be effective in helping these men and their families. I met one-on-one with officers; each had completed two to three tours of duty in Iraq and/or Afghanistan. Each had serious injuries, which would not allow them to return to combat, although they wanted to. They were informed about my visit and who I was, and each shared with me some thoughts and feelings about their experience. Gratitude was woven into each conversation for the others they had served with and those who had served before them. As I looked at these once healthy and strong bodies now maimed and, in most cases, altered for life, their heroism was palpable. I felt gratitude swell within me for their sacrifices. Yet these humble patriots stunned me with their generous expressions of gratitude to me for coming. Before I left each room, I asked if I could pray for them; not one refused prayer. As I took each hand and prayed, I was mindful to include the buddies they specifically mentioned in our conversations.

For these men and women in the armed forces, being there for fellow soldiers and for their country is their priority. However, we know that to fulfill this calling is costly. There are various losses involved such as loss of limb, mental soundness, and emotional equilibrium. Sometimes there is loss of life. Moreover, for every soldier serving in the military, there are those at home who wait, pray or grieve. Each soldier's life represents a group of people behind the scenes trying to carry on to raise and educate children, stretch finances, and cope with the realities of war. These sacrifices are real and challenging. They are protracted when a death occurs and grief is a daily weight. For those who have been touched by such a loss, the emotional toll is heavy. For those who have a peripheral view of these losses, reading comments by family members of soldiers allows one to enter into their grief.

Father's Day honors fatherhood and all that our dads do, and have done, to shape our lives. They include the fathers who are overseas now—or have been—who shape our country and shape character. Honoring dads will be as grand as special breakfasts of burnt toast or oddly shaped pancakes made by young hands that thrill a dad's heart. There will be handmade cards written in crayon as well as a multitude of carefully chosen greeting cards hand-delivered or mailed for a timely receipt. There will also be a longing for those who are not present to share the day. Absences may be due to military service, distance—emotional or physical—illness or death. For some, Father's Day will be one of bittersweet memories that stir emotions in unexpected ways. However, Father's Day is spent, for those who believe in God through Christ, every thought and feeling will be accompanied by God the Father's love.

The ministry of the Holy Spirit provides comfort, encouragement and support when memories or absence touch a heart. Be they good, painful, or odd remembrances, God the Father is present with each of us to help us comprehend matters in relationships and offer unspoken support. For the Christian, life's realities are not different than for those who live without faith in God. However, faith in God assures His presence and the advantage that one will never go through life's difficulties alone. God is there. Finally, faith in God's promises that because of Jesus, there will be a reunion one day with those we love who have gone ahead.

Fathers can be acknowledged on all days for their gifts, contributions, limitations, and attempts to be a father. Their courage of character is evident on the battlefield and in the hospital room. It is easy to see this when they are coaching Little League or attending Father-Daughter dances. It is still there on days when they lose their tempers and ask for forgiveness or lose their jobs and still need to be needed. There are days when they are full of hope and faith, and times when life seems to get the upper hand and dads are depleted. Whatever the days bring, life and all its predictable and unpredictable happenings make dads what they are and what they are not. The God of all fathers accepts dads just the way they are. God loves and honors fathers—on their days of victory and days of defeat. God loves them so. May we.

Lord God, be with fathers today and each day. Strengthen their faith and their conviction to do what is right in Your eyes. Give them courage to stand for what is right even when it is unpopular with their children or in the culture. Be with fathers who miss their sons and daughters for reasons known to You. Thank You for Your abiding presence as their Father. With love in Jesus Your Son, Amen.

Chapter 4

Touched

If I may touch but His garment,
I shall be whole.

Mark 5:28

Scripture tells of a woman who had suffered for twelve years of a blood disease. She had been to many physicians and spent all she had on cures that did not work. But then she heard of Jesus. Heard of Jesus. Did not see Him or meet Him, heard about Him. Hearing kindled her faith. The Holy Spirit was on her already with a touch of faith and hope that motivated her to seek out Jesus. She planned to get near Him. She did not hope she would be whole. Scripture writes that she was confident. She went from planning to touch Him to planning to receive healing. And she got what she came for.

It is interesting to read Jesus' heart in this account. And Jesus, immediately knowing in Himself that the virtue had gone out of Him, turned around in the crowd and said, *"Who touched Me?"* (Mark 5:30). The Lord knew someone had come to Him in faith. How meaningful for us to be told in this verse how quickly and fluidly the offering of virtue, of healing, transpired. 1-2-3-done! Virtue is defined as conforming to moral and ethical principles: moral excellence, chastity, an admirable quality. Only Jesus can restore with His touch a body maligned or a spirit nearly dead because of inappropriate touch.

A plethora of sexual temptation and sexual sin plague our culture. One need not look far to see how the media, advertisements, and music are among that which feed the culture. A steady culprit is the Internet. Because of the Internet, access to pornography, prostitution, and pedophilia is widespread. Wrongful touch, criminal touch, results in pregnancies, sexually transmitted diseases, AIDS, destroyed self-esteem, destroyed marriages, and even suicides due to betrayal, shame, or guilt. In addition, alcohol and drugs are used to cope, to escape, and even as barter, all of which further complicate this scourge. This is a public view of this dark sin. There is another side.

The hidden underground of human trafficking in which humans are sold as slaves for sex, labor, or war is a prolific and profitable industry filled with vile sin. While human trafficking is more predominant in poverty-stricken countries and involves more women and children than men, we learn more about the economic return and use of humans in developed countries—including America. David Bastone's provocative book *Not for Sale* shatters the myth that this does not happen in America's backyard. It does. It happens in America, even with all of this nation's resources, sophistication, and education. Human commerce is a thriving business. Sexual sin, greed, and control drive it. This reprehensible use of humans reveals the evil touch that destroys souls and destroys hope. Satan's goal.

Every keystroke that initiates visits to pornographic websites, every date rape, every person sold through human trafficking for sex, labor or combat bring about individual and corporate loss. We are lessened as a civilization by the sexual sins in families and nations undeveloped and highly developed. When touch is used to violate, manipulate, or forcefully propagate and abort because of inconvenience, God sees. These sexual sins and criminal acts bring about losses and grief penetrating and seemingly irreparable. Because of Jesus, they are not. There is a deeper touch that still can and does purify sin to make it whiter than snow—the touch of Jesus. No sin, no matter how subtle or egregious, is beyond forgiveness and cleansing. It may take much time to bring about necessary changes; however, the atoning blood of Jesus shed on Calvary covers every sin there is. Jesus' sacrifice was for all sin for all time.

God created human beings in His image. Therefore, we are made of that which is precious and valuable, that which is inherently virtuous. God loves us. He bathes us in love on a daily basis from morning to night and wants nothing to taint or bar His love. He wants His children to absorb His love, return it to Him, and share it with others. The manner in which we do that differs depending upon relationships, personality, and life experiences. However, the Creator of love would have all exchanges of love and self be respectful, meaningful, and beautiful.

Centuries ago a woman in the Bible had the faith to reach for Jesus' garment to receive wholeness. She needed His touch. She reached out in faith and received healing. Her faith released His power. Jesus' same power is available right now. Where there has been defilement, degradation, and betrayal, there is the touch of Jesus Christ to heal and to restore. The risen Christ stands ready to be touched and to touch.

Lord Jesus, You purify. You heal. You make all things new. There were multitudes in Your day as there are now who need You. But dispersed in the crowd of humanity, only some are aware of their need of You. The woman who reached for Your garment is kin to those who reach for You today. Magnify the Word of Truth in a needful world so those ravaged by sexual sin and its malevolence come to You to be healed. You alone have the power to override the vile tactics of Satan. You are here to do that. May Your gentle and loving touch be known to those in need of Your safe touch. Thank You, Jesus, for forgiveness, restoration, and wholeness that You generously extend. May we be mindful we are made in Your image. May we be sensitive to respect ourselves and others as creatures full of worth and virtue—for You made it so. Amen.

Chapter 5

God's Math and the Economy

Gather up the fragments that remain that nothing be lost.

John 6:12

It is a privilege to travel. Over time I have greatly enjoyed extensive international business and leisure travel. Asia was a highlight as it was fascinating and beautiful. On one of my trips there, I toured the Great Wall of China. It is massive and its history compelling. As I peered into different shops for mementoes of the trip, it was not the grand statues or paintings of the Great Wall that captured my attention. Instead, it was a diminutive beautiful porcelain basket filled with fish. It sits on my writing desk. It is a charming and inspiring piece I purchased when shopping one morning while on a trip to China. The kind Chinese shopkeeper tried to direct my interests to larger pieces, which were lovely as well. I passed on them. It was the small piece that spoke to my spirit. It brought to mind one of my favorite Bible stories, the young boy who gave his lunch to Jesus. My porcelain basket is not empty; it is filled to overflowing with fish. To me, it represents the extra after many were fed in the feeding of the multitude.

A boy with his lunch, five loaves of bread and two fish; the boy offered it up to Jesus, and it was multiplied to feed a multitude—with plenty of leftovers. After everyone has eaten, Jesus said, 5 (John 6:12). The Bible says the fragments amounted to twelve baskets. I believe the extra did not stop there. We still feed on that meal and its spiritual nourishment. Similarly, forgiveness never stops at 490 (70 x 7 = 490); that lesson never stops. Only one leper out of ten came back to say thank you; this leper was singled out as a constant reminder. A widow gave two mites, her all; her faith continues to minister.

God's math is such that often less is more. Whatever objects or people He uses to illustrate the condition of a heart, His lessons have exponential value for every place and time. These stories have applications for contemporary times, for they hold ancient truths that cultures and trends cannot change. Small amounts of fish, bread, and coins served as objects God used to make and inspire much. These scenarios are provocative because they reap spiritual dividends for those who invest their souls and futures in the Kingdom of God. Such investments cannot be calculated and written in man's ledger; only God and His ways measure such investments.

Faith is easier when times are easier. Faith is tested when trials come. Often this is when the Lord can best form character. It is a time when faith can deepen and burgeon. These are times when faith can act, be remembered, and stored in the soul as a testimony to the Lord's faithfulness. Trials have the potential to create a reservoir of compassion from which others may draw. John D. Rockefeller, Jr. said, "Giving is the secret of a healthy life...not necessarily money but whatever a man has of encouragement and sympathy and understanding." God can use times of challenge in ways that allow people to continue to give of themselves. Money is only one form of giving. Finding resources within oneself such as time, kindness, forgiveness, sympathy, and encouragement, are forms of giving. Imagine the sum of baskets filled with the extras-of-self that accumulate in times of challenge, the extras one did not think one possessed.

Read a newspaper or watch a financial show to get a daily assessment and prediction about the economy. Analysis is one thing, certainty another. Only God knows what is to come. Given economic unknowns, it is wise to take hold of what is certain for those who believe in Jesus Christ. He is here. He loves you. He has given the Holy Spirit to you for comfort and counsel. He has given His Word filled with promises that He will keep. Assurance of this comes to the heart via prayer and time. God is God. Nothing man does or says can alter His position and His commitment to those who believe in Him and trust Him.

Grief will be felt during times of job losses, downturns in real estate, stock and bond portfolio fluctuations, relationships that conclude due to work changes and company closures. The way that a Christian accepts the present and looks at the future is with a measure of hope that can sustain one through a downturn. Such hope is beyond natural understanding and certainly beyond material substance. Whatever transitions occur in life involving a reduction in resources, God is there to offer the opportunity to make such transitions purposeful. It may not seem so at the time. But the Holy Spirit is at work to direct affairs such that the outcome has a purpose and shall fulfill God's plan. Count on it.

The time I saw the Great Wall of China was memorable and inspiring. Yet, it was the small porcelain basket that registered in my spirit and brought to remembrance the fact that God's power is vast. He does much with little. His power brings large results from small offerings.

Lord, You know the precise needs of each person. When personal or national economies are difficult, help us to be wise, patient, compassionate, and faithful. When fully assessed, may the fruits of our lives prove that trying times are actually ripe conditions to produce spiritual dividends from generation to generation. In Christ's Name, Amen.

Chapter 6

Off Key

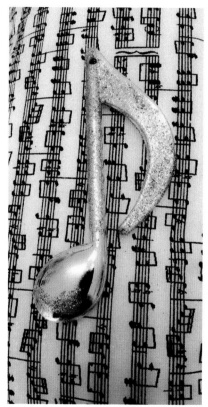

And I rejoice over you with singing.
Zephaniah 3:7

I cannot sing. Trust me. Oh, I enjoy singing: hymns in church, ballads, and songs from musicals all capture my attention. What I lack in talent I make up for in desire as I chime in and offer what I have—off key notes and all! However, when I am in the company of my young nieces, nephews, and godchildren, they want me to sing to them. So I do. Sometimes, they sing along, sometimes, they listen. They never hear the discordant notes I send into their young ears. To them, there is enough of a melody for them to sing with me or listen with enthusiasm. When I sing in their company it is as though I am not deficient at all in this particular talent. The reason why? Love.

When love is present, everything has a unique sound. Anything is possible. There are no limits. Endings are pathways to beginnings. Mistakes are covered with a cloak of forgiveness. It was love that brought Jesus from Heaven to earth—The Father's love for people. It was love that made Jesus obey God and fulfill His work on Calvary; Jesus' love for people made Him endure excruciating pain. That same love moves silently, boldly, and purposefully today to fulfill God's small and large plans for our personal lives—all of which feed God's ultimate plan for us to have a relationship with Him and spend eternity with Him.

God's profound love acts include help for those who wrestle with grief—persons who are unable to express love as they once did or who bear regret for not having done so when there was still time. When a loved one dies, God uses grief to tenderize a heart and make acute and clear memories and their worth. Yes, the past will bring tears, for either happy or sad reasons. But the Lord can take significant losses and use them to create a more meaningful relationship with Him. If we let Him.

For the Christian, Jesus is the center of all relationships. Therefore, He holds them together and brands them with His presence. When a relationship is infused with Jesus' presence and the Holy Spirit's touch, death has no power to conclude the breadth and life in a relationship. It goes on. Not as before but with a different kind of expression.

As with singing, when we love off key in Christ, it matters not. His love fills in the flaws. His forgiveness covers every mistake. His love is true and unrelenting. He loves not as humans love but as humans could love for *with God nothing shall be impossible* (Luke 1:37). In order to reach some of those high notes of loving others, one must first go lower in self to prepare for that higher standard. Not easy to do. But with daily effort, a desire to be closer to God, and relinquishing our ways for God's ways, incremental changes can and do transpire to deepen one's relationship with the Lord. Then improved relationships with others shall follow.

The Lord's love covers our sour notes. It balances out our offerings and continues to make a melody of our lives through and beyond grief, errors, regrets, lapses in judgment, and *every sin that does so easily beset us* (Hebrews 12:1) Our dear Lord and Saviour, Jesus Christ, makes it possible for you and for me to make harmonious the matters in our lives that without Him would remain discordant and flat. He raises our ability to love to the heights of His own simply because He wants to. No one else is capable of encouraging us to this level of love. Only God, through His loving Son, Jesus, can make such rhapsody.

Should grief tempt you to think you will always walk in an awkward direction and not regain harmony, think again. Remember the God and Christ of love, for they remember you. They know full well the sorrows of loss, and they are committed to staying the course with you through a difficult season that will eventually conclude. In grief seasons, go ahead and cry, recall, laugh, feel anger, reach out for help, and keep silent. Whatever means of expression you opt for at a given time while grieving is the way love may express itself. This can also be so even when one is not grieving. However odd expressions seem, be certain that God is with you. He will take everything that is off key to orchestrate a season He and you share that is rich in love—as only the Maestro of Love can orchestrate and redeem. May you rest in His faithfulness and assurance of love.

Father, loving us is what You do with perfection. Even when life hits hard and losses penetrate us, You persist in loving us through seasons of transition and pain. Lord, Thank You for Your tender yet stalwart presence that sustains and blesses. Thank You for the wonders of Your Son, Jesus, our precious and beloved Friend and Saviour in Whom we reside all our given days. In the resounding Name of Love, Jesus, Amen.

Chapter 7

A Little Bit Longer

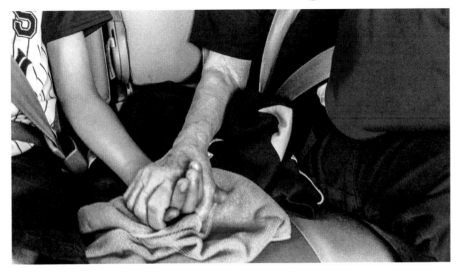

*So He shall give His angels charge over
thee to keep thee in all thy ways.*

Psalm 91:11

Sometimes when people pray together, they are inclined to hold hands. This may happen in a circle, when two people pray together or during a church service. In some churches, it is customary to hold hands while praying The Lord's Prayer. People reach hands across pews and aisles to pray. They sit at kitchen tables, restaurant tables, hospital beds, cars, weddings, funerals, holidays, and mealtimes.

TRANSITIONS

When people clasp hands in prayer, a common gesture is to squeeze the hand of another a little bit longer after *Amen* is uttered. There is a tendency to hold the hand of another person a little bit longer. That brief pressing of hands together is a human reflex that speaks about human ways of holding on a while more.

With every grace God gives to us, there is a desire to hold on. This life the Lord grants to us is one filled with people, places, things, memories, and dreams we hold dear. God wants it that way. He made it that way. Although this life is not the final destination for the Christian (Heaven is), during our earthly pilgrimage we get hints of everlasting life. The finest and warmest moments we know here can be likened to the Eternal Home where believers in Jesus shall live forevermore. Because certain people and experiences are so precious, we want to hold to them. It is painful when it is time to let go.

Grief is a season in life when letting go is in process. It is a sad time. It is an exhausting time. To say goodbye to someone or something and know that we cannot relive that season in life is to cross an emotional bridge of acceptance that may be one of the most arduous journeys ever taken. Sullen and long as days may seem, grief days are filled with enormous effort and energy; it takes much to adjust to a conclusion. Jesus knows this. Jesus stays through this process—just as He was there for the memory-making in the first place.

Believers in Jesus have an unbreakable bond with Him. Jesus holds all that we love—forever. Whether endings come due to illnesses, sudden deaths, divorce, miscarriage, empty nest, drug and alcohol abuse, or relocation, Jesus holds for us the essence of these relationships. He stores in His heart what is most meaningful. We are to remember that if someone or something is meaningful to us, the same is meaningful to God. Everything—everything—that matters to us matters to the Lord. He gives us life and its graces and He derives blessings from us as we share life with Him, in all of its joyous as well as sorrowful experiences.

When it is time for certain relationships and experiences to conclude, we try to hold onto them. We may be granted the time to linger. The Holy Spirit may bring inspiration to journal, write a song, create a painting or carve woodwork that helps adjust to goodbye. There may be times for prayer or silence that offer insights that speech cannot. The Holy Spirit may bring revelation through Scripture to comfort and strengthen. Whatever way one is inclined to express emotions and capture a time of meaning, the Lord is certain to offer a two-fold blessing. He will accompany us in the process of remembrance, and He will hold the future we cannot see in His heart of love and promise.

With Jesus, the future is certain. New life, a different life, is ahead. Jesus is the reason why hope is still real, even when it may not be felt. Jesus will hold on to you and to me in all of our times of transition, as we are inclined to hold on a bit longer to life as we have known it. He will keep His angels with us for protection. He will hold on to us with His incomparable, unbreakable, and unfathomable love. Trust Him to hold you. Jesus can. The Bible says so, and the Bible is the heart of Jesus.

Lord Jesus, You are the One who gives to us all the joys we behold in this life. You, Lord Jesus, are our reach to the future when we are too weak to hope. Lord Jesus, Thank You for carrying us through the beginnings and endings of our seasons in life so that we can fulfill our time in this world and know the many blessings You want to give to us. Because of You and Your promises, Lord Jesus, we can keep going on and believe in tomorrow and all of Your grace that still abounds. In Thee, Lord Jesus, Amen.

Chapter 8

Space

But God demonstrates His own love for us in this:
While we were yet sinners, Christ died for us.

Romans 5:8

Space travel is fascinating. For me, the intrigue began when I was a girl. My parents woke me up late one summer night to watch on television what my father said was "historic," and "you will always remember this." He was right. It was when Neil Armstrong walked on the moon. In July of 1969, he spoke those infamous words, "One small step for man, one giant leap for mankind." It was a miracle. The night left an indelible impression on me. The tears in my father's eyes were equally memorable. His emotion stayed with me. Admittedly, it was not until I was much older that I could appreciate this achievement and what my father understood that summer night: the study, expense, and vast details involved in space travel, and America's victories realized and tragedies suffered in the interest of space exploration.

In Buzz Aldrin's book, *Magnificent Desolation*, he tells of his life as an astronaut and the challenges he faced professionally and personally. When he describes his experience that summer night on the moon, one passage is especially stirring:

> I became all the more conscious that here we were, two guys walking on the moon, our every move being watched by more people than had ever before viewed one single event. In a strange way, there was an indescribable feeling of proximity and connection between us and everyone back on Earth. Yet we were physically separated and farther away from home than any two human beings had ever been. The irony was paradoxical, even overwhelming, but I dared not dwell on it for long.

Separation and connection between people are sometimes measurable by distance. However, it is via emotion that such measurements are more accurately assessed. When there is space between two persons due to miles, discord, or death, that space can be a welcome gap or an unbearable gulf. The sudden death of a child is a devastating loss for parents. Conversely, an elderly grandparent who dies after suffering from a degenerative disease is a loss that can bring a modicum of relief now that there is no more pain.

Relationships drive our lives. They are motivating forces that determine who we are to become in life, what we achieve, how we dream, and even what we hope to leave in legacy. As Christians, our relationship with Jesus is paramount. As sons and daughters of God, who we are to God and to ourselves is of high worth. Because of our great value to God, He does not want any separation between us. Sin separates. It is a barrier between God and people. Because this chasm exists between God and humans, God wanted to make a way to bridge that divide. Jesus is the way. Jesus is the only way, and the only One who can keep people safe in fellowship with God, free people from sin and shame, and bring people safely to eternity.

Resurrection Season is when we think about what it cost God and Jesus for our earthly and Eternal safety. In this reflective season, we think of Jesus in the wilderness as He prepared for that walk to Calvary. There He would die at the hands of men and sacrifice Himself for the forgiveness of all human sin. As we ponder the cross and Jesus' sacrifice, we may feel personal sorrow coupled with Jesus' sorrow. For those who grieve a loss, emotions in this season can be acute and seemingly without end. But there is an end. Because of Jesus, there is hope. Always hope. His submission on Good Friday and death on the cross looked hopeless. A black and bitter ending. But three days later Jesus rose from the dead. He did what appeared could not be done. He was victorious. Jesus is alive. Because He lives, you shall live.

Dark times come—in all forms. God knew they would. He sent Jesus, His only beloved Son, to go before us and beside us to be our Light and help in dark seasons. Whatever you face, the Lord Jesus is with you. He wants to accompany you through strange days. Let Him. May there be no space between you and the Risen Saviour— today and forever. This Lord of lords who created the universe and galaxies, who knows the pathways to the planets, stars, and the moon, loves you with an everlasting love. Jesus will guide you through your next day, next night, and next year. He promised. His rise is proof that He is with you. Trust Him. Let Him love you. Today. Every day.

Lord of Wonder, Scripture tells us that You were a man of sorrows and acquainted with grief (Isaiah 53). You carried the sorrows of human sins, and yet were propelled to do so for the sake of human forgiveness and hope. You did so out of love. Lord Christ, we embrace that hope. Thank You for the gift of Yourself given for our pardon, for the gift of Your love given because You do not want to live without us. We rest in the certainty that there is no space between You and believers in You. Creator of the Universe, blessed be Your Name forevermore, Lord Jesus Christ of Nazareth, Amen.

Chapter 9

Empty Nests

*All things were made by Him;
and without Him
was not anything made that was made.*

John 1:3

Don't blink! This was the advice of one dear dad to his daughter when she gave birth to her first child. In blinks—this is how fast the years go by. One day there are diapers, the next, the training wheels are off the bicycle, and next, they are launching out into the world and leaving home. College, work, marriage, relocation, and new relationships are factors that make for departures. While these activities are expected to occur one day, that one day becomes personal and often comes far too soon for parents who must now adjust to an empty nest.

Whether or not there are still other children and/or a spouse in the home, the absence of a child is a transition eventually made by all parents and siblings, as well. Natural brooders, moms are accustomed to having their young ones around. Natural protectors, dads feel a steady pull to guard. When these actions are curtailed, mom or dad can feel displaced—even in their own home.

When the nest changes and has been emptied of life as one knew it, the echoes of yesterday can be both rewarding and haunting. Reminders of days overwhelmed with raising a child, an array of inimitable memories, and pangs due to silence all make for what can be an uncomfortable and emotional adjustment. This is a time of grief. Sorrow, loneliness, longing, guilt, regret, and even anger can show up. It is worth recognizing that even happy departures are tinged with sadness and grief.

While there is often joy in seeing young ones branch out on their own, the reality of these actions spur feelings of loss. To be needed and wanted are powerful human pulls. When a parent no longer feels that same role is as full as before, grief can settle in. Growing into a new identity and new expression of that role as mom, dad, sister or brother will be different. However, it in no way minimizes the influence family members continue to have on those who no longer live at home. In fact, bonds can grow stronger. Distance will even offer the one who departed new insights and perspectives.

Empty nests also come about due to tragic and untimely deaths of young people. Such absences are grueling.

These losses are penetrating. They can challenge marriages. Often hope weakens when life is shortened by a homicide, suicide, or substance abuse. Unless someone has experienced tragic loss, it is impossible to know the depth of that grief. Those who grieve young people gone early from life are grievers who need tremendous support, great love, and much time to heal.

Childless homes can bring an undercurrent of emotion for people who long to have children but cannot. For some, the inability to have a family and participate in loving and raising a child can be an isolating experience. One may learn to cope, but sadness can strike when news of someone else's child is announced, when someone else's child celebrates a birthday, and when someone else's child is leaving home for adult life plans. There is a pang of sorrow that those experiences were never known.

The good news of Jesus' resurrection is that hope ascended when He rose from the tomb. That hope is everything. Every ending in the life of a Christian has an inherent resurrection quality. Jesus' rise gave birth to hope that lives and outlasts every seen conclusion and every lonely heart. The events in life that never happen and the events that do may bring sorrow, but they are also infused with an Eternal hope that God will continue to encourage and equip believers in Him to keep moving forward. New buds of purpose spring up, and the Lord transfers unique talents and personalities to new growth and opportunities. Because of God, there is always new potential to be realized. Always.

Scripture informs us that all things—not some—all things were made by the Lord. This means there is purpose in all He creates that is seen and concealed. Losses in life are painful as they come in different forms. But if one rests in God's promise to be with us always, that promise will not only uphold His saints as goodbyes are spoken, but will equally uphold the hellos and beginnings that await.

Lord Jesus of Life, You see it all. You are over the years of our lives to grant grace and strength to allow for remarkable and individual life tales that are our own. Lord, comfort those who miss someone. Give tender assurance that they are needed, wanted, and loved. Assuage any doubts, regrets or longing with Your presence that exudes hope and loving-kindness. In Thy Name, Lord Jesus, Amen.

Chapter 10

Spineless

*In the beginning was the Word and the Word was with God
and the Word was God.*

John 1:1

There is an old adage: A Bible that is falling apart usually belongs to someone who isn't. I knew someone with a spineless Bible, my grandmother. Her Bible was among the heirlooms I inherited when she was called home to Heaven. No spine at all. The pages are filled with notations, scribbles that make it all the more treasured. Her

Bible was her gem and companion; she read it with consistency and seriousness. I am still on my way to a spineless Bible. Among my Bibles is a slim one I have carried in my briefcase during my career. It has traveled many miles on trains, planes, and cars. The spine is fraying, but I still have lots of usages ahead to get it to its falling apart state.

God's Word was meant to be read regularly for all its merits. It stands triumphant from generation to generation. It has and it shall continue to stand the test of time. No matter the efforts to alter, edit, condemn, forsake, or dilute it, God's Word remains *rightly dividing the word*

> *So shall My Word be that goes forth from My mouth;*
> *it shall not return to Me void,*
> *but it shall accomplish that which I please,*
> *and it shall prosper in the thing for which I sent it.*
>
> Isaiah 55:11

of truth (2 Timothy 2:15). Its promises, warnings, consolation, and direction are immoveable and unmatched. This is God's heart. God's plan. Come what may, it stays the course. Distorted interpretations of God's Word cannot make it conform or perform to such interpretations. *God watches over His Word to perform it* (Jeremiah 1:12). God's Word works by God's power. Not man's. Therefore, it is still and shall always be the trustworthy volume to keep well fingered, highlighted, and dog-eared. It is the Book of books about the King of kings. It will continue to carry souls through this life into the life to come.

Seasons of transition can be extremely challenging times. A steady reading of God's Word aids in gaining strength and solace through times that bring grief and the need for healing. Reading the Bible is a cumulative practice. Each reading is a spiritual deposit to draw on in times of need. Regular reading of God's Word produces calm even when one is not necessarily seeking it. The Bible has a distinctive power to quell fears, offer understanding, and increase hope. People seek hope and help. Every day the Bible is the essential volume to know God, receive help, build faith, and combat Satan, the enemy of our soul. The Scriptures bring refreshment, rejuvenation, courage, peace, hope, and strength. God's Word is where to find necessary agents to bolster faith, bridle doubt, and regain perspective.

Aaron Jeffrey's inspired lyrics for "He Is" gives a brief descriptive summary of all sixty-six books of the Bible, depicting the richness and diversity of Scripture. For example, in Genesis He is the breath of life. In Exodus He is the Passover Lamb. In Leviticus He is our High Priest. In Numbers He is the fire by night. All the way to Revelation, where He is the King of Kings and Lord of Lords. Every line of the song and chorus is inspiring, and I highly recommend that you listen to it and immerse yourself in the knowledge that He is all these things and more: your Comforter.

No matter what kind of season or stage of life we are in, the Bible can and will take us through life and impart what we need at a given time. May we come to the Bible daily and throughout our lives to develop a spiritual spine and eventually hold a Bible that is so well-worn it becomes spineless.

Lord, Thank You for Your living Word. Holy Spirit, guide us daily to read the Bible and expect to read Your heart to receive wisdom, peace, and direction for our lives. May the lifelong reading of Your Word strengthen our spiritual spines and leave our physical bibles spineless; evidence of our habit and reliance on our closeness to You and the power of Your Word. In Jesus' Name, Amen.

Chapter 11

Forgiveness and a Shih Tzu

Then came Peter to Him, and said, Lord,
how oft shall my brother sin against me,
and I forgive him? Till seven times?
Jesus saith unto him, I say not unto thee,
until seven times but, until seventy times seven.

Matthew 18:21-22

Recently I was visiting my uncle and his good-natured Shih Tzu. I am an early riser so I got up about 5:00 in the morning, put on a pot of coffee, and decided to take the dog out for a walk while the coffee was brewing. This happy little dog investigated the landscape and meandered about as he usually did. He stayed near me, and eventually he was ready to go inside and began to go up the steps into the house. Suddenly he stopped and began to chew on what I thought was a foreign object that could be harmful to his body and digestion. I spoke to him and then I tried to take it from his mouth. He did not like that. He nipped at my hand, something he had never done. I stood there and watched him; soon he stopped chewing the object and wanted to go in the house. The family has been cautioned that while this little dog is friendly, one thing he does not like is to be disturbed when he is eating. But in this instance, I disturbed him in the interest of his well-being. He did not know that. Time would reveal that thankfully whatever he ate did not make him sick. He was fine.

When we went back into the house, he followed me around calm and happy. But I was unsettled. He might have bitten me! This was out of character for him. He knows me when I come over and knows I play with him when he brings me his toys. He is accustomed to having me pet him and be attentive to him. Given how amiable he is, I was surprised he would nip at me. He did not break the skin, but for me, the matter broke our fellowship. But not for him. He went about in his usual manner with me. I admit that it was with some trepidation I petted him after he ate his food and drank his water. He followed me around while I prepared my coffee and puttered around the kitchen. Then he followed me as I took my coffee to the guest room and went back to bed to read for a while. He jumped on the bed, curled into a ball, and settled in for a nap. It was as though nothing ever happened between us. All was forgiven.

Pets have something to teach us about unconditional love and forgiveness. Jesus said we are to forgive 70 times 7. Creatures that become part of our family seem to have forgiveness down. For them to forgive is something they simply do. No instructions required. Do I forgive that easily? Do you? For us forgiveness may take time depending on the incident, the person. We can be reticent to interact with someone if there has been an offense. The Lord makes room for that but He still wants the end result to be forgiveness. No barriers. No barrier to create a chasm that allows Satan to come in and agitate all the more and get one to thinking that the offense is unforgiveable. Jesus will forgive anything. We are to forgive. He wants no barriers. He wants nothing to infect our hearts. Forgiveness is always a matter of the heart.

When we forgive, we become closer to Jesus. Forgiveness is not acceptance of an act that occurred but it is a pardon for it. Do we not all need to be pardoned at times? I do. Others need my pardon. They need your pardon. When we forgive each other, we keep our personal communion with the Lord and keep unity in the Body of Christ. This serves as a witness to believers and believers-to-be. Even if communion with others is from a distance, in the spirit realm there is no division. This pleases God. Whatever pleases Him surely pleases those who love God.

As with any relationship of merit, would we stop forming relationships to be spared the pain of disappointment or loss? We will fail each other. At one point or another. It may be a slight infraction or a colossal betrayal. We are human. We are imperfect. No matter how good our efforts to do what is right and best, there are times we will fall short. The Lord allows us to gain perspective from our mistakes. He makes forgiveness a focal point of relationships as part of that perspective—for all parties. God's kind nature is such that He wants restoration not only for the relationship but also to retain the blessing of memories made so they continue to be a source of joy and gratitude for having made the memories.

Sometimes when we have had a challenging day at work or school, to come home to the dog or any pet and their company is a healing balm. Not only are pets a source of comfort, companionship, and entertainment, they can be instrumental in molding our character. That is what happened to me. Who knew a cuddly little shih tzu would teach me a lesson about forgiveness? God knew.

Lord, Thank You for family pets. They are evidence of Your blessings. May we continue to be mindful of how important forgiveness is. Your Son Jesus went to Calvary's cross for the forgiveness of all sins. Help us, Lord, to remember His sacrifice and yield to Your ways as we forgive others as we have been forgiven first and always by You. In the precious Name of Jesus, Amen.

Chapter 12

Until Death Do Us Part

To him whom much is given much is required.

Luke 12:48

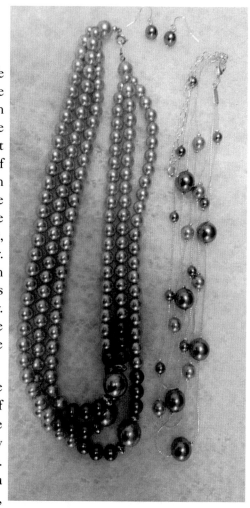

"Until death do us part" are sacred words. We have had either the personal experience of speaking these words or listening to them spoken at wedding ceremonies. Where these words take people is unknown. That is part of the mystery of love. From the moment of speaking vows to the time of the end of an earthly relationship due to death, is a unique and unpredictable experience. Some people spend many years together—decades of loving, changing, forgiving, growing, and growing older. Some people share a shorter span of time. When love is born and vows are taken, it is uncertain as to how many years a couple will spend together. When that physical union comes to an end, the grief it brings is an experience for which no one can prepare.

The ending of a marital relationship due to death is one of the most challenging kinds of losses. When two people unite their lives, the physical sever that death brings finds a widow or widower facing a maze of complex emotions. Years of building a life together and growing as a couple becomes a way of being. When that ends, life changes dramatically. Especially difficult can be the loneliness this loss brings. It can make one feel isolated, discouraged, and utterly disinterested in life. The future can seem bleak and even pointless. This is part of the depth of loving someone. However, this hollow feeling and gray view of the future is temporary. It will improve. Gradually. When until death do us part becomes a reality, those who love continue to live out *I love you.* Differently. But the act of loving most certainly continues during a time of grief. Finding a new way to invest time as one heals is still love in action. Those given the privilege of love also bear its responsibilities; healing is part of it.

Concentration on someone else's needs helps us bear our own. Working in a job, doing volunteer work for the church or community, and praying for oneself and for others are constructive. Time with family members and friends helps to round out life, and offers opportunities to share feelings and reminisce. Attending support groups, going out with acquaintances for coffee or lunch can be useful exchanges. Sometimes it can be advantageous to spend time with people who are not as close to the person who died.

Part of love is to endure the absence of a loved one and trust God. The path of grief is part of the path of love. Jesus promises to never leave one alone. While grief is painful, it does pass. It takes a long time and an odd route to heal. But healing does come. Life is different after the death of a spouse but life continues to hold goodness and purpose. God reveals the blessings still to be. Hearts can continue to hold gratitude for all that was.

It is of great value to remember that as we carry on, we carry within us a "pearl of great price." A soul. *Again, the kingdom of heaven is like unto a merchant seeking goodly pearls; who, when he had found one pearl of great price, went and sold all that he had and bought it"* (Matthew 13:45-46). When we get to Heaven, we will see how rich and beautiful God has made our everlasting life. Who could ask for anything more?

Lord God, You plan for certain people to come together in love and marriage to share life together. Because You know all that happens in our lives, You know losses in love will happen. Father, You sent Jesus to help in these times. Lord, grant those who grieve the loss of a spouse Your comfort and encouragement. Send ministering angels and wholesome company to their side to walk through days of sorrow. Restore hope for life and give meaning to the days. Help grievers live through their goodbyes and walk into lighter times ahead. This is asked in Your Name, Lord Jesus, and for Your sake. Amen.

Chapter 13

The Piers of Our Lives

*I love them that love Me
and those that seek Me early
shall find me.*

Proverbs 8:17

A pier is a platform from which we look out to new possibilities. Piers are beginnings, places where we stand at the edge of something that usually finds us expectant of a particular outcome. Among our pier-time beginnings are first days of school, weddings, graduations, new homes, whimsical days of summer, and new jobs. What is also there but hidden when we stand at these beginnings is the breadth of experience in them such as joys, memories, and accomplishments. This may include sad episodes and sad conclusions. A hopeful beginning may result in the loss of something due to natural fulfillment or a sudden death, divorce, illness, or storm. When we stand at the beginnings, we cannot see what is ahead. God can. He knows the entire length of our lives and every second of our lives. He knows what will become of our beginnings. This is why we are encouraged to seek out Jesus at the beginning of all our endeavors. He will be the constant on which to depend no matter how a beginning unfolds or concludes.

In late October 2012, Superstorm Sandy made landfall on New Jersey and ravaged the coastline of the Jersey Shore. Sandy's wrath extended to New York City, the surrounding region, and many states in the northeast quadrant of the United States. Flooding, destruction, and loss came and swept away life for many as it was known. People stood in shock after wind and wave had calmed and daylight revealed the enormity of the devastation. The storm was gone, loss and grief were left. Jesus remained.

Our lives will know loss. We can count on it. Loss is part of the human experience. Whether loss comes via traumatic events or planned departures, loss comes. Of course, dramatic events are far more challenging. Hurricanes, blizzards, expected or unexpected illness, death, fire, flood, income loss, and terrorism reveal that human life is fragile and susceptible to changes, including nature's fury and circumstantial shifts. We do, indeed, live on the grace and mercy of God. Daily. However, when we experience loss of any kind, hope in God's Son, Jesus, offers steady strength and companionship that is secure and unchanging. The Creator of all knows everything we will face before it happens. Therefore, a secure faith in Jesus will anchor us to face loss and transition with Him at our side. To trust our lives and the lives of those we love to anything but Jesus is to have a weak inner foundation that will wobble or even collapse. But placing trust in Jesus is to live on a sturdy foundation that allows us to begin again when life's trials and tragedies meet us.

Hope may be weak for you or someone you know due to dramatic loss or a life event that has shaken physical and/or spiritual moorings. Know that Jesus is strong. His hope for you is real and vital. Lean on Him. Jesus came to the world so that we would not be alone at any time in our lives but particularly in the times that challenge us. When we stand out on the piers of our lives at a beginning, Jesus stands with us. But we must consciously look to Him and desire His presence in order to be mindful of His love and strength at a beginning as well as throughout a new experience. He will accompany us, come what may.

Even if piers and plans crumble and bring us to new, unexpected views, He is there. We can trust Jesus. He is at our side. We can trust His strength to be our firm foundation and believe that there is still good ahead. All because of Jesus. Investing time in prayer and reading the Bible are ways that the Holy Spirit speaks and moves to bring comfort and guidance. These are ways that keep Jesus close. Wherever you stand today in your life, look at Jesus. Seek Him early in the thoughts of your days and the plans of your life. His eyes are fixed on you. He is loving, attentive, and trustworthy. Jesus will lead the way forward by His love. Trust Him in your every step based on His unchanging heart and complete ways explained in the Bible. With Him, hope is clear and near. Hope on.

Lord Jesus, life's changes can be abrupt or anticipated. It is difficult when we face these human challenges. But You, Lord, are our strength. With You and by Your abiding grace we live our lives. Help us, Lord Jesus, to build our lives with You by seeking You first. You are the only firm and lasting foundation. We shall seek You early in thought, prayer, and reading the Bible for strength, encouragement, and reminders of Your great love. You promised to be with us always. Thank You for always being there. In Your Name Jesus, Amen.

Chapter 14

A Parent's Loss

*Gather up
the fragments that remain,
so that nothing is lost.*

John 6:12

Natural or tragic deaths. Miscarriage. Divorce and custody contentions. Wayward sons and daughters. Addicted sons and daughters. Empty nest. Infertility. Estrangement. Gang membership. Incarcerated sons and daughters. Ill sons and daughters. These are some reasons (you can name others) that a parent or parent-in-longing experiences. The losses known to parents who face these transitions because of connections to children—

physical or emotional connections—are deep and painful. Parents who bear the strains of love for children or who desire to be a parent are strains Jesus understands. They are reflections of the power of God's love for the young and the unique endowment of love God places inside of people to love and parent.

Today's culture is a cauldron of temptation. This is especially true for young people and all living through this era. Drugs, alcohol, suicide, sex, bullying, cyber sins, and preoccupation with and influence by social media and other distractions are in the mainstream. These entice and threaten those who delve into these activities limitlessly and unadvisedly. The spiritual, emotional, and physical ramifications are significant when entering into these actions and choices. Sometimes they end in deep grief. Many bear the sorrows of self-destructive choices, the person who has made the choice as well as loved ones.

Loss hurts deeply. Loss requires time and attention to heal. Even so, the Lord's capacity of love inside of a parent is a treasure that has within it something new to give. In God's restorative power comes the enablement to love again in new ways and sometimes with new people. In the process, He takes the pains of suffering and weaves into it wisdom and strength for new love to rise. This is only possible through the power of the Holy Spirit. He truly enables a parent to keep loving. God gives to those open to it a new depth of love that cannot be denied. This is evidence of His love that is unending and unfailing. It takes a measure of courage to trust enough to love again. It also takes courage to keep loving and investing in those still here.

Whatever losses you have known as a parent or an onlooker to someone you love who suffers from parenthood or a desire for it, is a loss that can be healed by Jesus the Healer. Jesus has a way of getting inside of a heart such that fresh hope comes and possibilities present themselves. This is not immediate; immediacy would not allow for personal growth and deeper faith in Jesus to be cultivated. But, over time and quiet moments spent in God's Word and in prayer, God will make His presence known and offer strength to carry on. All He asks is that you give Him the fragments of your love. When you do, by His power and abiding love, He will see that nothing is lost. The Redeemer will redeem. Trust Him.

Loving Christ, You know the heart of a parent and the pains suffered due to loving a child and desiring to love a child. Lord, help those who bear emotional and physical pains as parents to know that You are with them. Lord God of Israel, You create children and bring them forward. Help those who grieve to know that Your love for those You create is greatest. All is in Your heart and in Your sight. In Christ Jesus the Redeemer, Amen.

Chapter 15

Taking Advantage of the Slope

Thou hast turned for me my mourning into dancing;
thou hast put off my sackcloth, and girded me with gladness.
To the end that my glory may sing praise to Thee, and not be silent.
O Lord my God, I will give thanks unto Thee forever.

Psalm 30:11-12

Miniature golf may seem like a gentle pastime, but the Spirit of God can use any activity to drive home a strong insight. This one day He did. It happened when I was playing miniature golf with my ten-year-old nephew. We were at the sixth hole, and he was leading the way through the course. After completing his swings, as I was getting ready to take my turn, he said, "Remember, take advantage of the slope." I did my best to yield to his counsel and completed the hole, but his words stirred me.

No doubt, he had heard this from his father when they play golf. He remembered it. Not only did he remember it, but he also applied it when it was his turn to swing, and he communicated it to me. Slopes, upward or downward slants, may not appear to be advantageous, in golf or in life. However, upon closer examination and the right touch, slopes can be of benefit when taking strokes. They can also prove instrumental in advancing us through the course of life.

When we suffer sorrow in life, emotions follow. Our sorrows can be slight or profound. Whatever the degree of sadness, it prompts feelings that can move us closer to God or move us away from Him. An experience that causes sorrow is an opportunity to see God's faithfulness and grow a deeper faith. Slopes in life direct us to go up or down. Tough times in life come with a slope; they can cause us to trudge up through a difficult transition and strive to get on even footing again. Or, they can look too high and too hard to navigate and prompt apathy, which sets in motion a stagnant or downward trend. For a while, this has its place because grief gives allowance for some lack of effort and fatigue. Eventually, we can see the trial of suffering as a test of faith. It is a time to employ everything we have believed to be true about God or hoped to be true. God will always prove Himself to be faithful to His promises. Staying the course of belief in Him will reveal His faithfulness to us in a personal way.

God loves you. God loves me. He wants each person to make it through life being dependent on His faithfulness. When we apply His promises found in His Word, we will gain insight and momentum that is supernatural and can carry us through to a better day, to a level place again. God has given us a book full of His strength and promises to be activated and applied. We make the strength of His Word and its inherent power a part of us when we read them and apply them. Trials are a primary time in life to accept His counsel. When we come through individual challenges, we reinforce the power of God's promises for the next time we face something difficult. Until we get to Heaven, there will always be trials at various turns in the road. But the God of Israel declares *I Am God, I change not* (Malachi 3:6). Therefore, His power to save is steady.

Miniature golf was an unlikely place to receive a nugget of truth from a lad. But it was a time to bear witness to the Spirit of God coming to offer a reminder about faith and building it up by taking advantage of slopes. How good to receive this reminder. In our every trial, we have the opportunity to experience the faithfulness of God.

Lord, You know our trials before we meet them and the pains that they bring. You feel them with us. You stay close to soothe and help us through the difficulties we face. You offer strength from Your Word. Holy Spirit, Thank You for staying at work in our lives as we negotiate slopes and when we are on even ground. Thank You for deepening our faith in all of life's peaks, valleys, and plateaus. In You alone, we trust. In Jesus' Name, Amen.

Chapter 16

Linked by Love

We love Him because He first loved us.

1 John 4:19

Construction paper. Glue. Paper lace doilies. Scissors. For many youngsters, these simple art supplies offer an opportunity to express love in a new way. The annual arrival of Valentine's Day prompts the making of a first valentine, a valentine memorable to a child and to a recipient. Such valentines are brought home and presented with great pride. Many a parent, grandparent, aunt, uncle, or friend accepts this particular valentine with glee. Truth be told, these gluey and crooked shaped hearts covered with a child's scrawl are more valuable than fine parchment with gold leaf. These valentines are priceless for the love they convey.

As children, adolescents, or adults, each age and stage presents us with different opportunities to express love. Unique personalities, talents, and skills guide expressions.

45

Each kind of expression etches a memory on a heart. These memories remain, even when people and circumstances change. As relational beings, we form all sorts of relationships. Whether short or long in duration, whatever is exchanged in love offers something meaningful to be remembered and stored. This is love's way. This is God's way.

God makes meaning out of whatever is shared. Exchanges in Him prove purposeful. When love is lighthearted and buoyant, purpose is clear. When relationships bring challenge, love's purpose is blurred. When relationships change or endings come, we can find ourselves perplexed. It may feel as though there is nothing meaningful happening or worthy to retain. But there is.

One day with the Lord is as a thousand years, and a thousand years as one day (2 Peter 3:8). For those who love, time is not. It has no measure for its capacity has no limits. With God, time is a continuum understood only by Him. Therefore, sometimes efforts for a beloved are not only toward a joyous hope; efforts may be to endure a sorrow. *I love you* cements the uncertain. Once a heart says these words, a host of unexpected and inexplicable events are sure to transpire. This is the way of life. Some events will be exhilarating. Some will be devastating. Devastations include death, illness, divorce, and discord. Coping with the underside of love is difficult. However, trials reveal love's depth and are often the catalyst that draws one closer to God. This closeness occurs during a stretch of time that will seem odd and maybe never-ending while grieving. But God has His reasons and shall guide.

For believers in God through Christ, every experience is known to God and held by God. Everything is shared in His presence, and each memory is preserved in His heart. Everything is linked by love. By God's love. God loved people first, and because of His love inside of you and inside of me, God makes it possible to link our lives to one another and to Himself in such a way that time, distance, disease or death cannot sever. Jesus is the link. Jesus is the proof of connection. Jesus' death on Calvary and resurrection from death is the ultimate revelation of love. Love is what kept Jesus obedient to endure pain because He loves you and me with all He is and all He has. Jesus keeps God and people connected to each other and to Himself—no matter what. Even the ugliest and most tragic endings possess something Jesus can use to change for growth and for God's glory.

Jesus Christ is the same yesterday, today, and forever (Hebrews 13:8). Jesus is the unbreakable link that stays and lasts. Whatever life brings, He is there. His love abides. His love renews. His love captivates. This love pours itself out in new ways in the interest of embellishment, growth or simple pleasures. There is comfort in knowing that Jesus is here, and He is unchanging. There is great comfort in knowing that He has the greatness to contain the best and soothe the worst that is exchanged and beheld in love.

Valentine's Day is set aside to declare and offer tokens of love. Candy, flowers, and especially cards are among the everyday objects given and received. Other kinds of tokens are more telling. Marriage licenses. Death certificates. Divorce decrees. Adoption papers. Passports. Deeds. Wills. Report cards. These are also evidence of love. These objects reveal how far one travels from the first expression of love drawn in a kindergarten classroom—travel that goes to the heights of serious commitments and realities far beyond doilies and glue.

Odd shaped valentines made by children fill hearts with joy, joy that serves as a prelude for more love to come. As perplexing as love's expressions can be as seen in changing relationships, would we ever trade them? By virtue of God's plan and His mysterious ways, it seems everything known in love has worth and is treasured—as treasured as those crooked handmade hearts.

Lord, because of You we know what love is. Because of You, our exchanges are forever valuable. All praise to You for the capacity You give to us to love. Thank You for comforting us when love hurts, when goodbyes come, when death's hour is known. Thank You for preserving the finest of all that is given in love. How grateful hearts are for all that we share with You. Life is rich in experience, which includes conclusions and transitions that sometimes hurt. Whatever comes, we trust You to be there and to link by love all the exchanges of our lives. In Christ alone, Amen.

Chapter 17

Final Hugs and Finish Lines

Wherefore, seeing we also are compassed about with so great a cloud of witnesses, let us lay aside every weight, and the sin which doth so easily beset us, and let us run with patience the race that is set before us. Looking unto Jesus, the author and finisher of our faith, who for the joy set before Him, endured the cross, despising the shame, and is set down at the right hand of God.

Hebrews 12:1-2

A runner awoke on the morning of the Boston Marathon with his mind focused on the race ahead. Not only was he a racer but also a husband and father. Much physical and psychological training went into his preparation for the marathon. When the big day arrived, thoughts were on completing the arduous run.

He ran the race and crossed the finish line. This man did not know that soon after, terrorists would set off bombs at the finish line that would kill his young son, maim his daughter, and critically injure his wife. The final hugs he knew before and after the race were celebratory. Now, the most grueling race of this man's life was about to begin: The race to survive.

Surviving a devastating loss is not accomplished alone. Many of us have faced sorrows and tragedies in our lives—or we will. Life finds each one of us coping with some kind of pain and loss in one season or another. Directly we meet with sorrow or indirectly when we enter into the grief of someone else and walk the path of grief. Surviving a loss and working through grief can be among the greatest accomplishments a life can know, for it begs tremendous concentration, energy, physical strain, and forgiveness. Such requirements are only met via the help of others who, through their ability to give, help each one of us to endure that which we must in order to survive loss and keep on living and loving.

Simple activities cannot be considered ordinary or endless. The routine hug in the morning when parting from children or loved ones, the spontaneous outing for ice cream on a weeknight, leaving work on time to make it home for dinner for no other reason than to be there, are indelible and cumulative activities. They do not get the focus of birthdays and graduations, but they rank high in memory making and fusing hearts for strong relationships. When time is taken for the final hugs in the morning and at night before going to sleep, that time may be the last. We never know.

The finish line that we run toward is the line that marks off the end of life. For some, that line is very far down the road. For some, such as a little boy cheering in the stands for his runner-hero dad, that line was closer than anyone imagined. More than that father could ever know, that final hug with his son would serve as a catalyst for him to finish the race of life, to strive to finish well. How? With hope and encouragement from others. The Bible encourages us that, throughout our lives, we have a great cloud of witnesses watching over us to cheer us on. That means we are being cheered on in times of victory such as finishing races and also when we trudge through times of grief. In God's continuum, He counts all the days of living as part of the race. He wants us to endure. We are already victorious through Jesus, the One who endured the cross to atone for our sins and give us hope. We look to Jesus for proof that we can go on by His example and His strength. Not our strength.

Jesus finished His course. He made it through life's sufferings. He did it for us. He wants you and me to stay in the race of life. Some days with footing strong, some days weak, but still moving forward. The Lord wants us to survive this life, for our sake and for those persons looking on from the clouds that line the skies as well as those of earth where others watch and bear witness to our continuing strides—no matter what. Jesus died for us so that we could keep on running the race of life. He has seen to it that we can indeed make it to the finish line for He is right beside us and serves as our steady companion. And when we do reach the end of life, we may be tired and tried. But we are certain to fall into the arms of Jesus, who by His powerful embrace will dissolve all human weakness and escort us into the light and endless joys of eternity.

Lord, You are the One who knows completely the sorrows we suffer. You promised to be with us always and carry us through difficult times. Thank You, Lord, for Your strength and touch that upholds and heals us. Holy Spirit, keep us mindful of daily activities burgeoning with life and love. May we never take our interactions with others for granted as You guide us on the narrow path to run our races and finish well. All this is asked in the governing power and Name of Jesus Christ, Amen.

Chapter 18

Later

But let patience have her perfect work,
that you may be perfect and entire, wanting nothing.

James 1:4

There was a time when *later* meant *later*, i.e., later on, later today or later in the future. However, in today's nomenclature, the word has morphed into a casual greeting for goodbye. Because later has lost its meaning, people are not inclined to respond to its directive to wait. Not waiting until later has consequences. Serious ones when driving while talking on the phone and texting. For some who do not wait until later to talk or text, later may never come.

This era of advanced technology allows people to communicate quickly. The equipment we have available at our fingertips and in the palms of our hands is mindboggling. Fast equipment, coupled with an accelerated desire to know, is a dangerous combination when operating a car, bicycle, boat, truck, any means of transportation. Even walking can be consequential, especially along bustling city streets teeming with pedestrians looking at smartphones, but not watching where they are walking. Clearly not smart. As humans, we may think we have it all under control and can multi-task to maneuver a car and simultaneously talk or text. We cannot. One blink away from the road can hinder reaction time; it could be the second necessary for attention to react to a situation to prevent a crash. Seconds of distracted driving can result in years of grieving.

Driving under the influence of drugs and/or alcohol have long been road concerns. Now, talking and texting is part of the mix. Many a parent, grandparent, sibling, wife, husband, daughter, son, and friend grieve deeply over the loss of life due to decisions that impaired judgment and took life away too soon. Tears of sorrow, acute anger, a sense of waste, and a dripping reminder of what might have been, accompany persons who bear the grief of losses that could have been prevented if someone had waited until later.

Sometimes a dramatic wake up call because of a near collision gives people a second chance. Sometimes not. For all of our high tech achievements, accidents due to human negligence are real. The cost paid in human resources, medicine, and finances is great. However, all of these combined do not come close to the toll taken on the hearts of grievers. Love always pays the highest price.

Jesus proves this. He suffered deeply for people when He went to Calvary. He took the sins of people on Himself, sins which include hasty and foolish decisions that inflict pain. Only Jesus understands the arduous pain of a mother who will not see her son graduate because he got behind the wheel intoxicated, the granddaughter who texted her favorite song to a friend and missed out on the music of her life, and the salesman who ran a red light to make an appointment and killed a mother because he was too engrossed in the sale on his mind and the phone in his hand. Distractions—silly or severe—can end life. Be it on roadways and waterways or in hearts, minds, and spirits. Only faith in Jesus can bring resurrection hope to those who trudge through grief because later was ignored.

God has shed much grace on us to live in a land where technology abounds along with the freedom to use it. He dispatches His angels more often than we realize to protect travels and guide us as we go to and fro. However, we bear a responsibility as new or seasoned drivers to be smart with phones in cars. This is our responsibility to God, to ourselves, and to others—strangers and kin—to preserve and protect life. Every person on the road is a soul God sees and a person with a life-plan the Lord has prepared. Staying off the phone—at every age—extends all life-plans.

One day in church worship I was seated near a grandfather and his young grandson. At the time to give the offering, we were waiting for the ushers to come around and I heard the little boy ask his grandfather, "Is it almost over?" His grandfather replied "Almost." I leaned over to the granddad and said, "That is equivalent to 'Are we there yet?'" We laughed. The boy was so quiet and well behaved one would not even know he was there. He had been observing and absorbing the steadiness of his grandfather, and it had taken root. Even though he was thinking about church service being over, the boy quietly waited until it was. Sometimes God uses children to remind adults to *Be still and know that I am God* (Psalm 46:10).

A hurried and harried citizenry is wise to consider the value of patience. Whether it is a glimpse of an obedient child in worship or an Olympic athlete exercising precise moves in an event for high marks, we all win when patience is exercised and better character is formed. Scripture informs us that patience will do its perfect work but that we must let it by giving ourselves over to it and giving God room to perfect our character. When patience performs its perfect work, we are told we want nothing, i.e., another chance to put the phone down on the road. God has an eternity planned for those who are in Christ but while on earth God wants us to see what other growth and blessings He has in store. To see His plans we have to wait until later. To let the phone calls and texts wait until later when driving is done, is to allow those plans to come into view. Your plans and the plans of others. Let us bring later back into vogue. Let us wait until later.

Father, You give us the ability to make advancements in technology. Thank You, Lord, for everything You give for communication that betters our personal and marketplace connections. Help us, Lord, to be patient and smart when it counts the most—in protecting life for ourselves and others by using technology in safe and undistracted places. May this bring glory to You and be a witness for others, young and old alike. In the Name of Jesus, Amen.

Chapter 19

The Glistening Christ

For unto us a child is born,
unto us a son is given;
and the government shall be
upon his shoulder;
and His Name shall be called
Wonderful, Counselor,
The mighty God,
The everlasting Father,
The Prince of Peace.

Isaiah 9:6

Jesus was born into this world of sin, pain, and challenge to save man, to bring joy, to bring hope. Without Jesus, there would be no hope. Without Jesus, there would not be—could not be—salvation. Jesus saves. Those who have trusted Jesus as Lord and Saviour shall be saved from sin and its penalties. Do you believe in Jesus? Have you asked Him to come into your heart and given Him your soul? If you have, I rejoice. If you have not—yet—I pray that you do.

Soon. There is still time to believe in Jesus. Time to believe in His love for you. Yes, *for you.*

Autumn of this year found me visiting the sacred 911 Memorial at the World Trade Center site in New York City. It was a horrific day of loss in America. The day I visited this site was gorgeous, a perfect autumn day of crisp air, clear skies, and bright sunshine. As I sat there to meditate, I recalled the tremendous daily activities that for so long took place on these grounds and in those former buildings. It was strange to now view this as solemn ground. This land that had served as a daily thoroughfare for commerce and commutation was no longer. It is now holy ground.

As I sat there, the Holy Spirit brought to my mind Ezekiel 37. passages of Scripture that speak of dry bones. Read it to review the entire chapter. In short, the question is raised, *Can these bones live?* Eventually. the response comes that the bones are to be prophesied over, and they are. Breath came into the bones, and they lived and stood up upon their feet, a great army (Ezekiel 37:10). These prophetic passages are deep and center on Israel, where Jesus was born. *Our bones are dried and our hope is lost* (Ezekiel 11). Oh, but there is hope. There was hope then, and there is hope now. Jesus is the living hope for Israel, America, and all nations. The lives lost that day are no longer part of our daily physical lives. This hurts. But at Christmas and throughout our lives, the reason for new hope rests in Jesus Christ, Saviour and Lord. Jesus was born to keep hope alive.

The glistening Christ glistens still. Destructive forces cannot destroy Christ. Death itself, a violent, slow suffering death committed at Calvary against Jesus of Nazareth, could not put an end to Jesus Christ. He rose. He lives. And because spiritual life and vitality are unending and continually renewed in Christ, anyone who believes in Him shall be filled with light and life. *"He that believeth on Me, as the scripture hath said, out of his belly shall flow rivers of living water"* (John 7:38). The reflecting pools at the 911 Memorial flow continuously. They are symbolic of the living water found in Jesus that continuously gives people a reason to hold on. Even when death strikes, when loss comes, and when hope weakens. Jesus shines His radiant light on circumstances. His brilliant presence and life-giving Word assure there is purpose ahead. The purpose may not be clear, but because of Jesus, *who knows the end from the beginning* (Isaiah 46:10), there is a plan for all that occurs. God's plan was for Jesus to come to us. God's plan is for us to come to God. Jesus is the way to God. The only way.

Life is changing dramatically in America and throughout the world. The tremendous changes taking place incline people to seek answers and seek hope. Jesus Christ is the answer to seek and the reason to hope. Celebrate Christmas. Recall dear memories and make new ones. Enjoy the blessings of gift-giving, special foods, and the merry innocence of children. As you do, be mindful that while the world changes rapidly, Jesus does not. His Word, His reason for coming to the world, and His hope for the world, are solid as ever. Be mindful of Jesus, who remains mindful of you. Christmas Day, sad days, every day, Eternally, He is the glistening Christ.

Glistening Lord, shine on us, in us, and through us. May the hope You bring renew our purpose. In Thy Name, Jesus Christ, Amen.

Chapter 20
Spiderman, Sandals, and Yesterdays

*To everything there is a season,
and a time to every purpose
under Heaven.*

Ecclesiastes 3:1

One morning I was out taking an early walk near the beach. At one point, I looked down and saw a tiny pair of Spiderman sandals. There was no one around, so clearly, they had been left from the day before. I imagined a drowsy toddler had fallen asleep in a dad's arms and was carried off the beach. I smiled at the small whimsical sandals. Perhaps the mom or dad had realized the sandals were missing; if they lived closed enough to the beach maybe, they could retrieve them. It made me think of a line in Robert Frost's poem <u>The Road Less Traveled</u>. *As way leads on to way, I saved that thought for another day.* Maybe this family went on to other thoughts, other roads. The sandals had their day.

We leave things behind. Knowingly and unknowingly. When seasons change in our lives due to death or the natural progression of stages in life, we find that there are items that are no longer necessary to keep. We clean out closets, jewelry boxes, carpenter benches, and china cabinets then discard various items. We thumb through personal collections and sift through memories that have brought us to today. We shed items. We retain items. Memories are connected to everything—memories frivolous and memories solemn.

When we go through the artifacts of yesterday and touch the past, we have the opportunity to leave behind parts of our yesterdays that are not meant to be part of now and the future. Letting go of some of yesterday makes room for today, for new experiences to be known and memories to be made. To go into the future laden with what was, leaves less room for what is and what is to be. *To everything there is a season and a time to every purpose under Heaven* (Ecclesiastes 3:1). To make the most of the seasons, we take what is ample for the next phase of life in order to see the next assortment of blessings God's want to give.

The Spirit of God has a way of weeding out the internal and external things of yesterday—if we let Him. The Holy Spirit gives nudges to us in times of significant transitions. Staying attentive and obedient to His nudges moves us along the path of change with His steady companionship. As Jesus promised, the Holy Spirit will always be there to direct us. When He is present, guidance comes, guidance that is in our best interest. When obedient to the Holy Spirit, we are certain to come through a life transition with deepened faith as we see the Lord's promises kept for us. We must turn corners in our lives to face what is ahead. Leaving behind yesterday can be painful, but God is with us. He is always there when we turn life's corners. We can count on it.

On a summer day, a child's Spiderman sandals were left behind. As children, teenagers, parents, grandparents, and adults, we leave things behind. As we do, we can trust God to bring to remembrance whatever He knows is of benefit for us to recall as we move forward. Transitions teach us that there are conclusions in life, sometimes difficult ones. Prayerfully we keep investing in the days with all that we have so that the best we leave behind is our witness to faith in Jesus, a testimony to the beauty of Him, and our ability to continue because of Him. This is evidence of the resurrection hope we have in Jesus. Jesus went all the way for us so we could make it all the way through life with Him. In the end, He promises we will reach a place where we know that everything had a purpose under Heaven.

Thank You, Lord, for Your generous heart and Your faithfulness throughout all the seasons of our lives. You fill our days with Your presence, the finest blessing we can know. Holy Spirit, help us and direct us as life changes and we go through various stages and transitions. Help us to release that which is best left as part of yesterday in order to open our hearts to what today holds. Lord, Thank You for the keepsakes that remain. They are reminders of Your grace, love, and tenderness. We love You, Lord, in all transitions. These prayers are lifted in the Name of the Saviour, Jesus Christ of Bethlehem and Calvary, Amen.

Chapter 21

So I Did

Ask, and it shall be given you;
seek, and ye shall find;
knock, and it shall be opened unto you.

Matthew 7:7

Earlier this summer, my little nephew and I were speaking about the Rainbow Loom bracelets he and his sister make. Last summer, when this craft made its debut and captured the attention of young children, my niece and nephew had the full range of supplies to become wonderful crafters with these small elastic links. I described to my nephew another color bracelet I would like, one different than the ones he and his sister already made for me. He said he could make it and that he would. We had not spoken of it again. I had forgotten about him creating me a new bracelet. I suppose I had presumed he had forgotten, too. Summer play and time moved along.

Then one day late in summer, there it was. He placed the beautiful pink bracelet on my writing desk along with a tender personal note he wrote to me in his young penmanship. I do not know which item means more, the note or the bracelet. I was moved by both and cherish them equally. The Holy Spirit stirred me, and I was given to consider the power of listening, and especially the listening heart of God.

Sometimes it takes a child to remind us that what we say is being heard. God listens to everything we ask of Him. Scripture tells us God wants us to come to Him and ask. Before we can receive, we must ask, seek, and knock. Then God can respond. Sometimes our requests are lighthearted; sometimes, we ask for serious help from deep within. He hears each prayer, weak or strong. He hears. He is faithful to answer.

"God is prompt to the moment," said Charles Spurgeon. When our requests to God result in Him seeming still, distant, and unresponsive to our prayers, we are wise to remember that God has reasons for everything. His timing is part of His reasoning. Grieving from a painful loss, going through an illness, and adjusting to life in new ways because of unexpected changes, are examples of situations that require time. Time is an essential component to bring us to where the Lord would have us to be—spiritually, emotionally, and physically. The Lord is always working matters out for our good (Romans 8:28). To God, our spiritual development is chief. If the Lord were to grant our prayers when we speak them, what dreadful results might befall us. God loves us so deeply that when He delays answers or brings answers forth in an entirely different way, it is because He knows this is best. That is what love does. It gives, always for the best outcome. Always.

Jesus showed His love for the Father and for you and me when Jesus went to Calvary and died on the Cross for our sins. That was an ugly act; it did not at all appear to be an outpouring of love. But it was. It was a sacrificial act of love. In it, Jesus covered our sins with His blood so that we would be forgiven by God. Our value to God is inestimable. Our souls and all else that make up our lives are never too small or great for us to go to Him and ask. His heart moves. His answers come. Wrapped in His love.

Exquisite is the little pink bracelet my nephew made of Rainbow Loom elastics with matching pink beading. It was a joy to receive it long after we first talked about it. What I did not expect was the pink beading that he artistically placed in the middle of the bracelet. I did not ask for that. An extra. A trimming. Something my nephew thought would make it more beautiful in appearance and richer in texture. It is. My handmade Rainbow Loom bracelet is now part of my treasure trove. Its value is not material as much as it is spiritual, and of far greater worth than human appraisals.

Keeping faith in the Lord is a treasure. Its value is beyond any kind of appraisal. To live with faith in the Lord and go along life's pathway is of immeasurable worth. If we say we have faith in the God who created us and loves us best and most, then we go to Him in prayer and trust He hears us when we pray. When God answers our prayers, perhaps a long time after we pray them or in ways we did not expect, it is as though He is saying, "You asked me, so I did." God's outcome will be refined with trimming and timing better than we can imagine. When God answers prayers that thrill us, and when He does not respond as we asked, three words ring out from every answer—*I love you.* He will only answer in a way that is best for us. That is what love does.

Lord God of Abraham, Isaac, and Jacob, You change not. Your heart is always listening to our hearts. Thank You, Lord, for seeing way up ahead as to how prayers are best answered for us. Help us, Lord, to have abiding faith in matters incredibly difficult. Touch us, Holy Spirit, with encouragement, patience, and wisdom so that we trust in the process of waiting for answers, answers with Your love threaded in for our best. In the Name of Power, Jesus Christ, Amen.

Chapter 22

Gratitude

Were there not ten cleansed? But where are the nine?

Luke 17:19

Jesus reveals much about His heart, our hearts, and gratitude in the story of the ten lepers. Jesus was walking through a certain village and the lepers were far off, far off because lepers had to remain on the outskirts and separated from others without leprosy. The lepers cried out for Jesus saying, *"Jesus, Master, have mercy on us."* They wanted healing. Jesus healed them. Each one. When they were healed, they went on their way—except for one leper. When this leper saw that he was healed, he turned back to Jesus, and with a loud voice glorified God, and fell down on his face at the feet of Jesus and gave Jesus thanks. Jesus asks *were there not ten cleansed?* Then blesses the one who came back to say thank you by saying to him, *"Arise, go thy way: thy faith hath made thee whole"* (Luke 17:19).

Only one leper came back to express thanksgiving. Glaring. Because Jesus questions the absence of the other nine lepers, we are wise to take notice. This story reveals the value God places on acknowledging Him for the blessing before moving forward in life to enjoy the blessing. Sometimes going back to say "Thank You" is a quick realization. Sometimes it is an arduous journey. This can be so when someone or something beloved is gone, and life will never be the same. Gratitude is easy when life is smooth and joyful. In the fullness of dreams, plans, and the living out of the routine and milestone moments, it is possible to meander along life's pathways ensconced in God's grace without recognizing God for all He has given. It is when someone or something we hold dear is gone that we may realize what we had—and then remember the Lord. The Giver. When the season for that blessing is over, two things happen in a heart—gratitude swells or bitterness grows.

People with gnarled hearts live with a resentment that is corrosive and cumulative. Because one suffers a loss that is cruel and/or untimely, bitterness can take root. Miscarriages, people killed by drunk or texting drivers, suicides, homicides, incurable illnesses, sudden deaths, drowning, those who perish due to natural disasters, and those killed in military service are among the reasons why people turn bitter on themselves and on others. They cannot find a reason that is rational nor acceptable. Accepting a loss, in whatever way loss meets us, is essential to healing.

Acceptance may or may not involve forgiveness. Not all losses are abrupt and tragic but every departure of someone or something dearly held involves a careful review of what has been with that particular person or circumstance. That review is individual for grievers because relationships are distinctive. What we develop with another person through an occupation, a sport taken away due to dementia or a maimed limb, are examples of relationships that define who we are. When that person or activity is gone, we ask, "Who am I now?" For those in Christ, identity does not change with a loss, but grief does make people vulnerable to good and bad influences. Sometimes if a bitter root encounters negative ground to which to attach itself, it will. Then negative thoughts and habits will creep in and try to take more ground in one's life. Anger is justifiable and often an emotion felt in times of trials. But anger that turns to bitterness is dangerous. Healthy anger subsides; bitterness may not. Jesus highlights the leper who came back to illustrate the importance of stopping to acknowledge the Giver prior to moving along life's way.

When we keep our eyes fixed on God as the source for everything we are given, it keeps us humble and dependent on His grace. Gratitude is a safeguard against pride. When we stay mindful of God as the source of all blessings, we reduce the potential for self-centeredness, self-elevation, and pride to take root in the heart. God hates pride. Satan does not. Pride is home base for Satan. It is what had him thrown out of Heaven. Satan was the most beautiful angel in the Lord's realm but that was not enough for Satan. He wanted all power and exaltation above God. There was not an ounce of gratitude in him for what God had given him and made him. There was the insidious desire for more. In God's economy, there will always be persons with more or less and the responsibilities associated with the measure He dispenses. However, when a hint of self-righteousness exists and expectation to be favored is present, pride is on display. Gratitude puts credit for blessings where credit belongs, with God alone. Pure gratitude plucks out bitterness and pride at its root.

Gratitude secures and deepens faith. When we are so moved by the Lord's blessings and favor on our lives that we come back to thank Him, we reveal our faith that He saw our need, and He heard our prayer. Moreover, thanking God after a protracted time of illness or grief, signifies God's faithfulness to us. His Word tells us, *"I Am God, I changeth not"* (Malachi 3:6). When we are in our difficult seasons, God is still all-loving, all-powerful, and all-knowing. He will bring us through tough times and lead us to the next seasons in life with an embellished character and more robust faith, which develops as the direct result of a trial. He gives insights and knowledge about Himself and life that we would never know without loss. Every loss brings a gain of some kind. It is wisdom to seek out what that gain is.

There is a song titled "Thankful" on Josh Groban's CD, *Noel.* Although this is a Christmas CD, "Thankful" is a beautiful and stirring song to listen to throughout the year. The lyrics include the following line, "And every day we hope for what we still can't see." Sorrow comes; it blinds us to what we cannot see. But hope in God is not a shallow hope, not the world's hope. The Lord's hope is alive even if we cannot feel it or see it. We may be unaware that God's hope is carrying us but it is. God's hope is the hope that does not disappoint (Romans 5:5). His Word says so, and God backs up everything He promises with His heart and His unequaled power.

This Thanksgiving will bring its share of blessings in traditional cooking, baking, football, and activities common to this holiday. For some of us, the day will be quite different than previous years if we have experienced a serious loss. There will be pangs of missing and physical pain for those enduring illness. Jesus understands. The Holy Spirit stays close to comfort and to reduce and relieve emotional and physical distress. The Lord is continuously present, loving, and compassionate. To know this and take each breath in the certainty of His presence and His promises is to live with hope and healing. Life will not be as it was. But it is still filled with faithful God who gives us grace and responds to the cries of our hearts. Nine lepers went their way after receiving a blessing from Jesus. One leper was made whole because he came back to say "Thank You." In all that we must let go of in this life, to hold on to gratitude enables us to hold on to love. This Thanksgiving, and each day, may we turn back to Jesus to say "Thank You," and then look ahead with the assurance of His grace and blessings to unfold.

Lord Jesus, we come back to You today to say Thank You for Your touch on our lives that has produced abundant blessings. We come back to You today to say Thank You for hearing our prayers and seeing the tears of those who suffer in any way. Lord, we know You care and You respond to those who call upon You in faith. We gladly give to Thee the glory and the honor for all o the blessings our lives have known and shall know. We trust by faith that even sorrows You will refine into faith more precious than gold. This we pray in Thy Name, Lord Jesus, Amen.

Chapter 23

V8 or Ginger Ale

We love Him because He first loved us.

1 John 4:19

For those who have helped someone who is quite ill, the simplest of requests are those we want to meet. On Valentine's Day, I was with a beloved family member whose illness made him thirsty. Frequently, he asked me to get him V8 or ginger ale, the only beverages other than water that the doctor permitted. His ability to swallow was weak, but the taste of these liquids was welcome and refreshing. When I would put the cup to his lips and help him swallow, his countenance became joyous. His thanksgiving and sincerity were generous for these little sips of relief. My cup runneth over for the grace to be able to hold his drinking cup.

Valentine candies, fancy hearts, and decorations adorn shops and advertisements in the month of February. St. Valentine's Day is an opportunity to express love but not in the simplicity of V8 or ginger ale. However, it is often in the common and everyday activities that we truly see the beauty and depth of love exchanged. Hearing the voice of a grandchild on the phone, being greeted by the dog at the end of the workday, receiving a text from an old friend, and seeing the familiar face of someone who puts a glow on our face, speak of love. These are among the common yet treasured experiences in a day that make life worthwhile. And these are also a sampling of the reasons why the absence of them makes life so challenging.

When illness, death, estrangement, divorce, addiction, and other relational separations occur, there is a void in life that only Jesus can fill. He is the One, the only One, who can make up for the emotional or physical distances that hurt. Jesus is also the One to credit for having known such good moments that live on in memory. Jesus heals. He helps us to believe in life and cherish what was. Where the Lord is resident in a heart, it beats with true love that lasts and lives on. Whatever may or may not occur with relationships that have changed, the Lord will not change. His ways are trustworthy. Jesus and His love are here to stay. Calvary's Cross and His resurrection are our proof.

Those who believe in Jesus recognize the Bible as a love letter. In it, the Lord declares His love and promises of love. Changes in our lives and relationships will not change His heart toward us. This is valuable to remember. Jesus stays. His love is fixed on you, on me. He wants us to count on that love. Eternally.

The next time you greet the dog at the door after work, linger a bit longer to pet him. The next time your son or daughter calls, stop multi-tasking, and listen. The Holy Spirit will give you something special to say. The next time you sit beside a loved one to help nurse an illness, have your Bible handy and choose a few passages that bring comfort and hope. When it is your turn to ask, "May I get you a V8 or ginger ale?" drink in the moment yourself. This moment is both common and divine. Remember the good in love with gratitude. Leave uncertainties to God in prayer. Live in God's love and grace—while it is now.

Lord, Your love for each person is deep and complete. No expression of Your love for us is insignificant. Therefore, when You place love in our hearts for each other, no expression of that love is small. Thank You, Lord Jesus, for the opportunities we are given by You each day to fulfill small loving acts for someone we love, to be recipients of the same, and have the gift of memory to hold close. Thank You, Lord Jesus, for Your heart in the Bible and for Your momentous act of love—dying so others could live. We love You, Lord Jesus, every day and every season. You are why we love. You always will be. In Your Name Jesus, Amen.

Chapter 24

Blind Faith

Thomas, because thou hast seen Me, thou hast believed;
blessed are they that have not seen, and yet have believed.

John 20:29

On Sunday morning during worship, the ushers directed the congregants on the left side of the church into a line to receive communion. A couple who raise puppies to become seeing-eye dogs for the blind took their place in line, bringing the puppy with them in accordance with training protocol. As the pastor offered the elements to the couple, the dog looked up at the pastor and softly whimpered as if to say, "I want the blessing, too." The trainers of the dog gently ushered the little fellow back to the pew.

The puppy's training prepares him to lead a blind person who will become dependent on this animal's skills and instincts for safety and guidance. These dogs make it possible for blind persons to work, go to school, and live a productive life because of the training and protective instincts of these dogs. As part of the puppies' training, they are never given food and treats as a prize for doing something well. Instead, they are always given love. Trainers will reward the puppies with kindness, petting, and hugs. Because the trainers themselves have big hearts and loving homes, the puppies learn quickly about love. When love is received, love is returned because it is modeled. These dogs become exceedingly affectionate companions to the blind people they serve and their families. The blind persons come to trust these dogs, a trust established out of mutual necessity and the consistent responses by the dogs.

Blind faith is essential when difficult seasons come and life's pains are deep and debilitating. Grief is one of these seasons. It can be one of the loneliest and darkest times in life. The loss of a loved one and/or a dramatic change in circumstances that sever us from what was, can bring us inside caverns of emotions we have never known. We may think we are to navigate all this alone. We are wrong. Jesus is right there. Not only does He remain in dark and sorrowful seasons, He knows the way through them and out of them into the light. He is the Light. His promises are never more trustworthy than when we have to live out the promises for ourselves. Once we walked through a personal valley and have owned the truth of His faithfulness, doubts often diminish and trust builds.

Think back to the telling of the appearance of the Lord Jesus after He rose from the dead and went to see His disciples. He met with Thomas, who doubted this was Jesus. Thomas wanted proof that this was really the One who had gone to the Cross on Calvary to shed His blood for the forgiveness of sins. Thomas required evidence. The scars on the Lord's hands from when He was nailed to the Cross were the proof Jesus offered, and Thomas accepted then proclaimed, *"My Lord and my God"* (John 20:28). Jesus provided the physical proof Thomas needed, but the Scripture above indicates Jesus added that there is a blessing for those who believe without physical evidence.

Blind faith looks to the heart of God and what He has said in His Word, not to the details of circumstances to find assurance. The Lord wants us to stay dependent on Him—when things go smoothly in our lives and when they are filled with challenges. Years ago, when I was on a writing assignment for an organization seeking to find jobs for blind people, I needed to shadow the social workers for meetings with blind individuals who were candidates for jobs. I learned there are two types of blindness: congenital, existing from birth, and adventitious, which is accidental and comes later in life. Depending upon when a blind person became blind, some had the ability to know how to function in certain situations because they had some sight at one point in life. If blind from birth, they had to be thoroughly dependent on others so they would not bring harm to themselves or others.

In many ways, the foundation of our faith is developed from what we are given at birth as well as what gets molded into our faith from life experience. Faith can be keenly developed in times of weakness because God's strength is our only means of support. A weak spirit and body yielded to God can be upheld with His strength. But a weak spirit and body given over to anyone or anything other than God cannot stand the test of time. There are all sorts of barriers humans use that prevent the operation of faith in God. But the Lord is of great patience to wait and to woo so those barriers vanish. Yielding to the Lord and the movement of the Holy Spirit are certain to yield blessings, strength, and hope for tomorrow. However faith is cultivated, via congenital or adventitious means, it is wise to extract every ounce of experience from life that makes faith grow.

The little puppy in training that peered up at the pastor in the hope of receiving communion whimpered for not having received the same blessing as the people. What this young canine did not know was that to his trainers, the blind person he would eventually serve, and fellow worshipers in church, he was already blessed, and he was a blessing. Furry and feathered friends that greet us at the door after work, cuddle with us on the sofa, or fly over to us and perch on our shoulder are ones we fuss over and enjoy. Pets become family. The gentle acts of affection we exchange with them strengthen the bond we share and provide warm moments of living and giving. Their unconditional love and silly ways bring us laughter and make our lives richer and our homes warmer. Unconditional love shared with people also make our lives rich and our hearts full. What a way to live.

Lord, make us instruments of Your peace. Where there is hatred, let us sow love; where there is injury, pardon; where there is doubt, faith; where there is despair, hope; where there is darkness, light; where there is sorrow, joy. Grant that we may not so much seek to be consoled as to console; to be understood as to understand; to be loved as to love. For it is giving that we receive; it is in pardoning that we are pardoned; and in dying that we are born to Eternal Life. Amen.

—The Prayer of St. Francis

Chapter 25

The Price of Memories

The memory of the righteous is blessed.

Proverbs 10:7

The Wall Street Journal recently featured an article about the history and hopes for the costume worn by the cowardly lion, Bert Lahr, in *The Wizard of Oz*. The classic film celebrates its 75th anniversary, and one man seeks to take advantage of the focus. The owner of the 60-pound lion skin had put it up for auction at Bonhams Auction House. He hopes for a seven-figure bid.

The sale of the lion skin will enable its owner to expand his museum in California that features Hollywood nostalgia. In addition to the cowardly lion costume, he owns Burt Lahr's script with the actor's handwritten notes and "Play It Again Sam" piano from *Casablanca* starring Humphrey Bogart and Ingrid Bergman. The sale of the costume will enlarge his collection and maintain the other items he rotates from storage units in California.

Most of us have our top ten list of favorite movies. *The Wizard of Oz* remains on mine and still holds first place. When I was little, I recall that whenever *The Wizard of Oz* was to air on television, it was announced several weeks beforehand. It typically aired at night, and that meant my mother and father would let me stay up past bedtime to watch it, even if it was a school night. Those were days before you could record a broadcast. If you wanted to watch it, you had to be right there in front of the television. I was. My mother would make special snacks, and our family would watch the movie together.

At the end of the movie, when Dorothy hugs her little dog, Toto, and says, "And, oh, Auntie Em, there is no place like home," I would always cry. My mom and dad would smile affectionately. What a comforting feeling to go to bed after the movie was over and feel the love of home and family. As much as those childhood memories mean to me, what happened as an adult stirs me also. When I was away college, and then when I had my own home, the movie was aired only once a year (before cable television), and I would watch it. At the end of the movie, I would get a phone call from my mother and father asking, "Are you crying?" in a warm way. I was. We would laugh over my tears. They knew that even as an adult, the final scene went straight to my heart.

Seven figures for the lion's costume? Quite a sum. But there is not a price high enough to match the value of precious memories a heart holds. Physical symbols mean much, and we all have sentimental items that trigger memorable times and places. Dear as those items are, what lives inside of us is beyond measure. At Christmas, we are especially sensitive to the memories we have made with certain people. We are also mindful of making new memories to be added to the life story that it is our own.

Christmas, other holidays and routine days may be challenging when life changes, and certain people no longer share our lives for reasons such as death, estrangement, dementia or military service. Their absence can be painful. Longing for what was, laughter remembering times gone by, and pangs of regret, can surface at different times—unbidden. Jesus is the One, the only One who can take our yesterdays and make them meaningful. He does what His Word says He will do, *work all things together for good* (Romans 8) and have them make sense and be purposeful. Some memories are wonderful; some require the synthesis of the Holy Spirit to bring them to maturity and acceptance. The Lord knows what is needed for each of us. By faith we trust Him to work things out for our good.

If I had seven figures to shower out donations and meet needs of many kinds, I would have lots of fun. There are people and organizations I would get a thrill out of blessing. Acquiring a famous cowardly lion's skin would not be in my plans. But someone out there may have a deep purse and a spirit that would like to own the costume. As for me, my childhood and adult memories of the movie, and my parents and their love for me shall forever glow in my heart and be more than enough when I think of *The Wizard of Oz*. For most of us, the glow of memory is the priceless treasure we get to keep, a treasure that seven figures or higher could never buy.

Lord of Bethlehem, we come before You humbly and thankful for all the grace You have given to us that lives on in memory. Thank You for countless memories of love. We pray Your peace and comfort for those who do not have warm memories and for those who grieve. Because You came down to us from Heaven, we celebrate Your closeness and rest in faith that one day we will be with You in Heaven, and with all those we love that You called Home before us. Until then, Thank You for the gift of Your Presence, salvation, memory-making in this life, and the grand tomorrow promised to all who believe in You by faith. Thank You for Your promise that the memory of the righteous is blessed. In You, Loving Jesus, Amen.

Chapter 26

Yet

But let patience have her perfect work,
that ye may be perfect and entire,
wanting nothing.

James 1:4

Yet implies hope. When a sentence ends in *yet*, it offers possibilities to be discovered, lived into, something to be fulfilled. For example, "They are not home yet," makes one think they are on the way. "She has not developed that skill yet," implies that study and practice continue toward developing a certain skill. "They do not believe in God yet," but we pray for them to receive His love and gift of salvation. The last sentence is especially thought provoking when individuals reject God and His love and/or deny that God has the power to turn around one's life or a situation of importance. This can be particularly hard territory to navigate when someone has been terribly hurt or betrayed by someone dear or by life's circumstances. God may get the blame.

Healing from a loss of any kind brings a challenge. When belief in Jesus is not part of that process, the challenge is exacerbated by the Holy Spirit's percieved absence and the supernatural power He longs to bring. God thoroughly understands why people reject Him, over a lifetime or for a season. He has complete knowledge of the state of every heart, and can pinpoint the moments in a person's life (even if many years have passed) when one deliberately or subconsciously began to pull away from the lure of God's love. Grief and the pain it brings can pierce like a dagger's edge. While people may have legitimate anger and dismay over certain losses, God's love is the antidote that gently and precisely touches the wound to bring healing and hope. But it is that very divine love that can be rejected and clustered into the same human love that leaves a heart disappointed and distant from God and others.

Sometimes a rejection of God is not due to pain in life but the result of never having been introduced to God personally or not having given thought to a need for Him. For some persons who have moved along in life without a relationship with God through Jesus, God is a word not a Person; church is a place, not a place of worship. Prayer is something someone else does for them, but they do not do for themselves or for others. God understands. But it is often this same person who may become vulnerable due to an unexpected life circumstance and then a need for God is stirred. God is eager to meet that person and that need.

God's patience is not our patience. His quotient for waiting far exceeds that which we are capable of matching. God can see down the road of years, even to the exact moment when someone will surrender their life to Jesus as Saviour and recognize their need for Jesus to save them from sin, from shame, from a life and Eternal Life without

Him. Arrival to such a moment is ushered along by prayer. Prayer that does not give up. Prayer that hopes. Prayer that avails much because one takes God at His Word.

Each of us has lived through seasons of challenge. Or we will. No life is exempt from a certain measure of difficulties. If someone has not yet yielded to God and taken to heart, step, and life the substance of God's Word, its solace, warnings, and promises, then prayer is the action to take for their sake. For now. Placing prayers at the foot of the cross and into the heart of God is to pray with belief that, while someone may not have received Jesus yet, hope lives. This hope remains an encouragement for those who intercede in prayer and for those whose names echo in God's throne room. Yet, it is indeed a hopeful word. No one holds out hope more than God Himself, for God's Word states *the Lord is not slack concerning His promise, as some men count slackness, but is longsuffering toward us, not willing that any should perish, but that all should come to repentance* (2 Peter 3:9). The beauty of God's love is that His yet extends until the last breath of one's life. Hope remains steadfast for those who have not turned to Jesus— yet.

Lord God, Thank You for the power of prayer. It remains the single strongest act that a Christian believer can practice in order to move people closer to You. For those who do not know You yet, Lord, we pray another day does not pass without their belief fully invested in You. For those who ache in isolation because they have not asked You to enter their seclusion, we pray You will touch them and then burst forth in their hearts to bring faith, healing, and ardent hope into these lives. And for those who do believe in You, Lord, may each one hold firm to their faith, as You remain true to Your promise to never leave or forsake Your own, to be with us always, even to the end of the age. All this is prayed in Your perfect Name Jesus, the One who sacrificed everything in death so all who believe in You can have everything You intend in life and in life everlasting, Amen.

Chapter 27

What If You Had Not Given of Yourself

*Guard thy heart with all diligence
for out of it comes the issues of life.*

Proverbs 4:23

Several years ago during the holiday season, I was asked to go to Walter Reed Army Medical Center to meet with wounded soldiers returning from war in the Middle East. The officers had fulfilled at least two tours of duty; it was highly unlikely they would see combat again due to injuries. I was asked to meet with them individually to talk to them, pray with them if they wanted prayer, and give them copies of my book, *Seasons of Goodbye*, which could help them cope with some of the losses they were facing due to fellow military members dying and/or personal injuries. Of the many places I have been asked to visit and speak, visiting soldiers at Walter Reed made an indelible impression on me.

During one of my conversations with a wounded officer, he explained his reason for voluntarily enlisting: September 11th. He was deeply impacted by the attack on the World Trade Centers. While watching some of the footage, he felt compelled to enlist and do all he could. He was a young, humble, and intelligent man who had fought courageously and willingly in the Middle East. His concern was that he was not still over there. He very sincerely said, "I have to get back to my buddies; they need me."

This man was seriously maimed. Without God performing a miracle, he would not engage in combat again, and his civilian life would be significantly altered due to his injuries. As I looked into his eyes, his intention to return to battle was earnest; the abundance of his heart was speaking what he wanted to do—make a difference for others. He seemed to be waiting for me to encourage his hope. Knowing that in all likelihood that was not possible, I said to him, "What if you had never gone? What if you never gave of yourself at all?" With that, his eyes opened up, and it was as though a light went on inside of him. Something registered. An insight perhaps that he had made an investment and what he had to give was given. He had the physical and emotional wounds to prove it. Now maybe he also possessed the internal satisfaction that comes with having no regrets. The tears in his eyes and his soft words, "Thank you for saying that," let me know that God had just imparted to this man a measure of healing and relief.

Time is precious. Couple this dear commodity with good health, and you have the makings for living well. And generously. Not in the giving of things as much as in the giving of self. Tangible items are sometimes the result of giving, but extending the gift of yourself penetrates others in a way that nothing material can. We may never know how our gift of self changes a life, changes a decision to a positive one, changes the course of someone's direction toward good and away from evil. But unless and until we opt to offer what we have, we block changes for ourselves and others. These are changes God wants to make for us from our offerings of self.

Often people think themselves unworthy, unskillful, ungraceful, or unprepared to offer anything of merit to others. As human beings we all fall short of perfection. As Christians, we are a work in progress, but never without the guiding and equipping presence of the Holy Spirit to work through us, for us, and for mutually beneficial outcomes and part of the craftsmanship of God's perfect plan. With the Spirit's leading, we give what we have and leave the results to the Lord. We may not go across the world as a soldier to give of ourselves. It is the distance we travel in the heart that tells.

Much is exchanged at Christmas. At Christmas and always, God is looking at our hearts. What we give of ourselves to others we are really giving to God. In His loving way, He makes our offerings to others return to us in fullness of heart and peace that nothing material can match. Christmas may be different for some of us this year as we miss people who are no longer part of our lives. Some of the most profound healing from loss can come when we give of ourselves to someone else. The Holy Spirit can use small or large portions of self to make us more like Christ, which is the finest return from giving of ourselves.

Cards. Gifts. Visits. Phone calls. Emails. Text Messages. Dinners. Lunches. A simple cup of coffee. Common activities, yet they all hold opportunities to give. What if you had not given of yourself? Your heart will tell you the answer, one way or the other.

Lord, Christmas places our focus on You and on matters of the heart. Love is why You came to us, died for us, and now live for us. Lord, may the fullness of Your birth, life, death, and resurrection make us mindful of Your heart that shows us how our hearts can be when yielded to You. Help us, Holy Spirit, to find creative and useful ways of expressing hope and encouragement to others as we give of ourselves generously and, in the process, are filled with the love of You. This we ask in Your Name, Lord Jesus, Amen.

Chapter 28

Replacements

*God will wipe away
every tear from their eyes.*

Revelation 7:17

Recently a dear old friend called me. We talked about Christmas preparations and that she, her husband and daughter had just finished putting up the Christmas tree. However, she left the top bare. She explained that the angel that sat at the top of three for nearly thirty years would not adorn the tree this year. It broke in her hands when she took it out of the box. It was fragile; because it had seen many Christmas seasons, it was worn with love and use. Her daughter attempted to glue the pieces together. The angel is somewhat together, but not strong enough to be put on the Christmas tree. Thus, the top is bare—this year. There were tears when it broke. My friend has not been able to replace it. Her heart is not interested in buying a replacement. "Why am I so upset over this piece when we have many other beautiful pieces to use instead?" she asked. My answer—because it was not an angel that broke in your hands, it was your history and all the personal nostalgia it represented.

She remembered vividly when she bought it and where she was. At the time, she was with her grandmother, a dear lady who died many years ago. She gave thought to different homes this angel had seen over the years and how her family would create new memories with their heirlooms as the years unfolded. This angel had known various attics and basements where it spent time in its box in storage until the next Christmas season came around. Given all the history it made along way with keeping family and memories connected, no wonder there were tears when it broke and could no longer be placed in its annual spot atop the tree.

This angel is irreplaceable. This is true of all objects that hold personal meaning and value to us. At Christmastime, our senses are keener. The traditions and people with whom we are linked come to life anew as homes are adorned, preparations are underway, and yesterday and today meet. When we bring out those boxes filled with our yesterdays and the people associated with them, they do initiate some tears—even without breakage. The mere sight of an ornament is powerful. It can bring one to times and places in such a way as to suspend time. Sometimes this can hurt since lives change. Family members and friends die or move away. Those objects serve as solemn reminders of what has been. They are also objects that renew hope and touch hearts with gratitude for what was. Because of the life in them, when they are damaged, lost, stolen, burned in a fire or worn by age, it may be necessary to spend a season with no replacements. If and when such inclination comes to replace items, we will know it. One day we may be ready to attach ourselves to a new object, new person, new pet; then there will be the openness it takes to meet life afresh, knowing there are more memories to be made. But even when we add on, the old that is gone remains part of who we are and where we have been.

For those who believe in Jesus Christ and all that His arrival in the world means for time and for eternity, there is a hope that transcends losses, earthly disappointments, and broken angels. This hope comes via confidence in the Saviour, Christ the Lord. Belief in Jesus, weak or vibrant belief, assures eventual arrival in a place where every tear shall be wiped away. For those who have yet to believe in Christ as Saviour, it is my sincere hope that this is the Christmas when that belief ignites. We will suffer losses and challenges in this life. But in Christ, who has overcome the world, His power is above loss and life's sorrows. In the incomparable scope of Christ's love, there is mystery and purpose in and beyond broken hearts. May the gift of Christ's irreplaceable love— love that heals and sustains—be yours this Christmas and Eternally.

Lord Jesus, Thank You for being with each and all for whom Christmas is painful this year, for reasons fully known to You. May Your loving touch console, revive, and encourage spirits. Lord of Bethlehem, we worship and adore You at Christmas and forevermore. Amen.

Chapter 29

Thoughts on Pet Loss

So God created the great creatures of the sea and every living thing
with which the water meets and that moves about in it, according to their kinds,
and every winged bird according to its kind.
And God saw that it was good.

Genesis 1:21

Years ago, a colleague walked into my office one morning clearly distressed and disoriented. We were getting ready for a major presentation, and I could tell she was out of sorts. When I asked what was wrong, she tried to shrug it off and said it was nothing. Eventually, she told me she felt silly about her emotional state; it was due to her dog's death. Once she said it, the tears flowed. We talked for a bit, I got her a cup of coffee, and she composed herself for the business meeting. After the meeting was over, she told me she was embarrassed by her grief over her dog. I looked at her quizzically and said, "But he was a member of your family." With that, she said, "I never realized it before, but he was."

Our pets are family. They become part of our daily activities out of necessity or playfulness. It is easy to get accustomed to their presence and habits. Anyone who has or who has had a beloved pet knows that pets have distinctive personalities. When we live among each other, little things happen that tell us they know our habits as we know theirs. We laugh as we come to expect them to respond to us in certain ways. Is it any wonder we mourn their passing and grieve when death takes them from our lives and our homes? Separation can happen when natural disasters strike. Pets are sometimes lost, and the inability to be with them at their end is a more complicated grief for there is no closure or memorial. Indeed these creatures are members of our family.

In the breadth of God's amazing love He is marvelous in the way He enjoys variety. He shares His creatures with us and invites us to delight in them as He does. Our pets— furry, feathered, or slimy—are creatures God gives to us to care for and to be cared by. Yes, pets care for us. How? Simply by their presence as well as their dependence on us to meet their needs. In this way, we feel needed. I recently learned of a young man who had been challenged by life for various reasons and wound up taking in a dog for a neighbor who could no longer keep him. That little dog's dependence on the young man made him feel needed in the world. That tiny animal served to give encouragement and initiative to someone who had been searching for a sense of belonging. God allowed one of his little creatures to care for this young man. There are no coincidences in life; everything is by divine movement and appointment. Surely, God arranged meeting this need via a Chihuahhua.

Have you lost a pet? Does someone you know grieve the loss of a pet? Do not think it silly to grieve an animal. God does not think so. Tears and grief are signs of love. Love and grief are related. If we love our pets, we will cry over them and remember them. We will find ways to memorialize them either in backyard ceremonies or pet cemeteries.

Certain songs have lyrics that stir us, and one of these songs is, "When You Say Nothing At All." The writer of this song, Ronan Keating, likely did not have his pet in mind when he penned it. Nevertheless, the lyrics are beautiful and speak of trustworthy love. It is a favorite song of mine. When I began to write these thoughts on pet loss, the song came to mind immediately. Perhaps the Holy Spirit would like it to serve as reminder about pets and their love for us, love from creatures that say, *I love you* without words.

Refrain from "When You Say Nothing At All"

The smile on your face lets me know that you need me.
There's a truth in your eyes that says you'll never leave me.
The touch of your hand says you'll catch me if ever I fall.
You say it best when you say nothing at all.

Lord, in Your infinite generosity You give to us relationships of many kinds. The people we hold dear who are with us now or in memory are gifts we cherish. Pets are gifts from You that we treasure. The seasons we spend with beloved pets are time we value and miss when seasons change. Lord, be with those who grieve the loss of a pet. Give to them the sweet touch of memory and guide them in a meaningful way to remember their pet, that special family member they love. Thank You, Lord, for all the relationships you grant and sustain. We trust all our connections in Christ Jesus our Lord. Amen.

Chapter 30

Time

To every thing there is a season, and a time to every purpose under the Heaven.

Ecclesiastes 3:1

Jesus came down to sit beside man
so that one day man might come up to sit beside God.

Time—it passes. Sometimes quickly. Sometimes not. Its passage quickly or slowly is often entwined with our hopes and expectations. When we anticipate something special, time moves much too slowly. When something is ahead that we would rather not face, the hour comes too soon. In truth, time moves at its usual pace—whether we are ready for certain experiences or not.

For some, Christmas is a season long-anticipated as loved ones reunite with those home from military service. It will be welcome by those who rejoice because they are given a gift of a clean bill of health. Then there are those with new babies who will celebrate their first Christmas. As always, there are many children filled with glee as they anticipate the joys of Christmas as only a child can view them.

For some, this season will be met with reluctance and tears. Loved ones who gathered together may no longer be alive. There are loved ones who may not be together due to divorce or estrangement. Relocations for jobs, homes made in new cities, military service and the miles of separation will make Christmas less joyful. Illness, economic strain, and various challenges in life can make Christmas a difficult day. Oh, but Jesus. Jesus is the reason for Christmas. Jesus is still the reason for hope.

Jesus came to give hope. Not the hope that humans can conjure or material holidays can bring, but hope that is spiritual, lasting, and complete. Without Jesus one truly has no hope. With Jesus, one does have hope; perhaps weak, but it is Jesus Himself who keeps hope alive. Not you, not me. Only Jesus.

Whatever view you take of time this Christmas season, take time to be with Jesus. Do not let the activities of the season or emotional reluctance keeps you from your time with Jesus. Jesus is the peace-giver and the hope-giver. Rest your days in Him this Christmas season. Raise your sights afresh on the One who keeps hope raised for a world in deep need of hope. His love never fails. His hope lives. Let His love and hope wrap around you so that time does have worth. So that He can make the time count. Your time. There is no one else in this world like you. You are unique, and you still have something to give and to receive. Allow Jesus to be the friend He wants to be to you. From His arrival as a baby in Bethlehem all the way to Calvary's cross, Jesus had you in His heart. He still does. Hold on to Jesus. Jesus is holding on to you. Let Jesus sit beside you today and be your friend. Your very best friend. Truly, He is.

Lord Jesus, thank You for the precious gift of hope that You give to us. Your arrival in this world signifies a joining with us so that we would never be alone. May hearts be filled with Your hope this season. By faith, may all of life's circumstances be entrusted to Your care and Your view so we can carry on in hope. In Thee, Lord Jesus, Amen.

Chapter 31

A Matter of Respect

*Greater love hath no man than this
that a man lay down his life for his friends.*

John 15:13

While on a vacation in Cape May, New Jersey, I witnessed a *Lowering of the Flag* ceremony that takes place at dusk. Vacationers in Cape May are familiar with the tradition. It is primarily geared toward teaching children about the flag, patriotism, and honor. Typically military veterans are asked to participate in the ceremony. One lovely summer evening when I watched the ceremony conducted, a question was asked which I could hear. After the flag was lowered and being folded, a young child chosen from the assembly to assist the procedures asked one of the military men, "How come you cannot let the flag touch the ground?" and he replied, "It is a matter of respect."

Flag Day comes and goes each June, yet many of us have an American flag flying outside of our homes all year long. We do. It is a symbol of patriotism and remembrance that signifies freedoms we hold dear, freedoms that have cost human life. American military defends freedom and allows us to go forth in our sacred liberty.

A matter of respect is why the flag is honored. It is a symbol of respect we uphold for those who fought for us—and fight for us—near and far. Freedom is costly. It is not maintained without a price. A high price. Some lay down their lives to defend America and other nations. People grieve because of loved ones who have died in battle. Some pine for dads and moms far away who are not there to see firsthand the prom dresses, graduations, and Little League games. Individuals who serve our nation by wearing a military uniform give their years of service and pay with their hearts. So do those they love.

Jesus came into this wounded and needful world to be the ultimate sacrifice that saves us from our sins and from an eternity separated from Him. Jesus' death on Calvary cost Him everything so that you and I would have spiritual freedom and everlasting freedom in the blessed home of Heaven. Jesus is our risen proof of giving all that He had and giving up His life for others. Sometimes our military, law enforcement, firefighters, and EMT's have to give up their lives. As the flag is lowered in Cape May, at military bases, and at every funeral, we remember their sacrifices. The United States came into existence with sacrifices, and requires still more to maintain the nation. We look at our flag and remember all it represents. We look at the Cross and remember Jesus, the Saviour who died so that we could live in utter liberty—forevermore.

Lord, Thank You for the men and women everywhere who defend the United States and the freedoms we enjoy. Jesus, You gave Your all so that we could be with You forever. Thank You, Jesus, for all that You did. Our liberty is in You—in this life and everlasting life. Your sacrifice for us out of love for us is clear and cherished. Our love overflows. In Jesus' Name, Amen.

I pledge allegiance to the flag
Of the United States of America
And to the Republic for which it stands
One nation, under God, indivisible
With liberty and justice for all.

Chapter 32

The Strategic Holy Spirit

The thief comes to steal, kill, and destroy;
I come that they might have life,
and that they might have it more abundantly.

John 10:10

In grief seasons, emotions fluctuate, and a generally reliable sound mind becomes less so because grief can fog the mind. Clouded judgment and unpredictable emotions are part of the grief experience. Escapes to ease the pain of loss is a choice people may not recognize as potentially serious problems. Drugs, alcohol, and other forms of addiction can take hold. What is reached for as a temporary balm can become a habit. A destructive habit. To oneself and to others. It is wise to consider that grief seasons make one vulnerable and vulnerability can bring harm. Grief distorts reality and thrusts into a new reality because of losing someone or something of personal value. Adjusting to that new reality is often difficult and takes time and energy. Grief is an exhausting process, and as time passes, people sometimes come to participate in pseudo forms of healing that can wreak more havoc than offer cure.

In the classic hymn penned by Martin Luther, "A Mighty Fortress is Our God," he dedicates part of the hymn to the truth that there is another who possesses strategies to possess souls. The devil. The devil is an enemy of the soul, a deceiver whose motive is to ruin lives and take souls captive. Jesus has defeated the enemy of the soul. The ancientness of this adversary cannot override the might of the Ancient of Days, a name given to Jesus who has proven power far above the strategic plans of the ancient foe. Martin Luther's insights prove valuable as the words bring meditation in a time when many people reach for drugs. Opioids especially. It is an epidemic in the United States because of its low cost and easy access. The weakness grief brings can make one reach for drugs in a vulnerable moment, and then come to live out the hard truths that accompany an unwise choice. It is good to yield to God in every choice, to reach for the heart and hand of God and trustworthy people, to pray, to make the enemy flee. In a weakened state, one word can send the devil away— *Jesus* is the word.

Greater than all other persuasions is the strategic, purposeful, and powerful Holy Spirit. He guides individuals in accordance with God's Word. His strategic moves are filled with love and protection. This is the good news that assures the steady and reliable presence of God. Grief is hard enough without having to battle an addiction that only produces greater pain and deeper regret. Sensitivity to those in grief is necessary during the rawness of grief when loss is first known, and also for the ongoing process of grief. Being sensitive to those who grieve helps a person come out on the other side of grief whole and without additional weights and sorrows, possibly stemming from unwise choices made while grieving. Praying with and for someone in a grief season makes an enormous difference for the griever and the one praying. The strategic Holy Spirit will help to compose prayers, silent or spoken, short, or long. The strategic Holy Spirit will guide thoughts to help persons who grieve make careful choices so that step by step and choice by choice they come out on the other side of grief with hope and a newfound purpose.

Holy Spirit, thank You for being with all those who grieve. Your strategic movements make for a wholesome process through loss that can bring one to deeper faith. Thank You for the inspiration You gave to Martin Luther to pen words that remain still valuable to us now. We lean on Your power and follow Your safe and sturdy lead. All this is prayed in Jesus' Name and for His precious sake, Amen.

"A Mighty Fortress Is Our God"

Martin Luther

A mighty fortress is our God, a bulwark never failing;
our helper he amid the flood of mortal ills prevailing.
For still our ancient foe doth seek to work us woe;
his craft and power are great, and armed with cruel hate,
on earth is not his equal.

Did we in our own strength confide, our striving would be losing,
were not the right man on our side, the man of God's own choosing.
Dost ask who that may be? Christ Jesus, it is he;
Lord Sabaoth, his name, from age to age the same,
and he must win the battle.

And though this world, with devils filled, should threaten to undo us,
we will not fear, for God hath willed his truth to triumph through us.
The Prince of Darkness grim,
we tremble not for him; his rage we can endure,
for lo, his doom is sure; one little word shall fell him.

That word above all earthly powers, no thanks to them, abideth;
the Spirit and the gifts are ours, thru him who with us sideth.
Let goods and kindred go, this mortal life also;
the body they may kill; God's truth abideth still;
his kingdom is forever.

Chapter 33

Notions

God placces our tears in a bottle.

Psalm 56:8

It didn't look like much. In fact, it appeared to be too ordinary to be practical. But my grandmother said it was, so it was. Whatever my grandmother believed to be right and good, it had to be. So when she referred to a zigzag-shaped seam binding to be sewn on the inside of a dress she was sewing, I shrugged my shoulders, watched her work, and knew that it was part of the plan. Once the garment was completed, I could not see the seam binding, but it was firmly placed underneath to reinforce the hem and to complete the garment correctly.

Whenever my grandmother, an expert seamstress, talked about items she required for her sewing projects, she spoke of notions. Notions included seam binding, buttons, thread, and needles, various yet necessary elements to hold a garment in place and make it serviceable. When my grandmother and I were out shopping and she was choosing her various items, notions were on her list. I found myself eager to look at the fabrics, and see the colors and patterns of fabric bolts. But she would look at the totality of a project, not only the fabric. Even when she was choosing the pattern and fabric, notions were essential to the process, and she included them in her design and planning.

The Bible tells us that God *places our tears in a bottle* (Psalm 56:8). He saves them. He saves our tears shed from sorrows and afflictions imposed upon us and/or self-imposed. He captures and contains them. Tears do not evaporate. When we weep, we dry off our faces and carry on. But the liquid proof of our pain has been lodged in the storehouse of God. In Revelation, we are told *the Lord will wipe every tear from our eyes* (Revelation 21:4). Could it be that the collection of our tears will be poured into Heaven's crystal sea and turned into living water that flows unto God's glory? Water is a powerful sign that God uses. Our tear-drops are relevant in this earth realm; in Heaven they are kept to withstand time and remain secure with God.

What notions are to sewing projects, teardrops are to the faith life of a believer in Jesus Christ. In God's estimation, tears are quite valuable. Tears are cohesive. They connect to the heart and all things true. Everything that touches the heart of God's children touches God's heart. God sees the tears cried. He feels the pain and knows why we cry. Losses in life produce tears. Sometimes tears are deep and riveting, sometimes soft and quick. Whatever the reason for tears, the Lord blends the experience of sorrow with His Spirit to bring comfort and refine character into the likeness of Jesus.

This process to console and strengthen through life's losses can happen multiple times in an individual life. Coping with loss will not cease until we are in Heaven with the Lord. Only then will we comprehend the depth of development that it took to produce a likeness to Jesus, which is God's overarching goal for each of us. Expressions in life are essential to build us, i.e., tears, laughter, trials, decision-making, grief, faith, obedience, trusting God, and even disappointments, serve to fulfill God's plans. In the process, *God works all things together for good for those who love God and are the called according to His purpose* (Romans 8:28). The God of perfection and purpose knows how to do this—and He shall.

When my grandmother finished sewing a garment, the seam binding could no longer be seen. Similarly, when our seasons of tears pass, we enter a different season, and tears that once were are no more. However, the tears that fell are held in trust by God. God does all things well. Knowing that God has captured our tears and holds them can only mean that we never cry alone or in vain. God knows and heals. He is loving and wise. He is with us. His Spirit is our handkerchief. His promise is our balm.

Lord, Thank You for making it clear in Your Word that You see tears that flow and You use them and save them for Your perfect purposes. Our lives are a walk of faith. We learn that the hardest trials often produce the deepest faith and lessons. Lord, please grant strength and peace to those who hurt and shed tears. Send a spirit of encouragement. Be glorified in our tears, and be glorified by our continued walks of faith as You perfect us on the journey. All this is asked in Jesus' Name and for His precious sake, Amen.

Chapter 34

Tables of Grace

*He is before all things
and in Him all things hold together.*

Colossians 1:17

Where do we begin to express gratitude for all the blessings in life? For those who have accepted Jesus as Saviour, Jesus is first in our hearts because *He is before all things and in Him all things hold together* (Colossians 1:17). Everything of worth is in Jesus. This fact does not change when lives change; especially when losses, disappointments, and set-backs bring emotional challenges that blur reasons for gratitude. Losses in life can do that: dull vision and expression —for a time. Gradually it comes back. Not as before, but little by little, there is a new ability to see the Lord's faithfulness in times of change.

Thanksgiving is a time of year to ponder the truth that our giving God never changes even when our lives do. God is The Great Giver who is always with us. Facing life without someone we love means that grief touches us. Memories of Thanksgivings gone by and pangs of missing are real because of the beauty and joy shared while creating memories were real. When special occasions come and certain people are no longer there, apprehension can accompany holidays rather than happy anticipation. God, our Giver, sits beside us, as He always has.

God knows the tables of grace that we come to because He prepares them. These include Thanksgiving tables as well as the many kinds of tables we sit at throughout the year. Other tables of grace include the laughter over coffee with a friend, dinner with a college student who is swamped with coursework and missing home, breakfast with a military father home on leave, feeding a baby in a high chair as he plays with toys on his tray, and feeding turkey and stuffing to an elderly patient in the hospital. God is at all these tables. He is present each day and season of our lives, not only on the highlighted occasions but every day. Why? Because God loves you and me. He wants to share life with us. That means the lighthearted days and the heavyhearted nights. Come what may, God is with us at the tables of life. Because He is there, His Presence makes them tables of grace.

There is much to be thankful for as I look around my life, even though it looks different this year because precious people have died. Yet bushels full of memories remain, which grow more treasured with time. What also remains is the embellishment of character woven into me because of these extraordinary people and the gratitude for all the tables of grace we shared while we were together in this world. Faith in Jesus assures reunion—a reunion where we will sit at His banqueting table.

It is my hope and prayer that this Thanksgiving season you look around at your life and consider the many tables of grace where you have been seated and the people with you. Some people may still be in your life, some may not be. For certain, God is still with you. May you be with Him and sensitive to the year ahead and all the tables of grace where you will sit. Humble or posh, God is there. May we remain mindful that each day we have the opportunity to make a memory with God, the Giver of our tables of grace.

Lord, as we ponder the many blessings that You have given to us, may You be blessed by our thankfulness. In times of change or steadiness, be glorified in all we are, and all we are becoming because of life's transitions …more like You. In Jesus' Name, Amen.

Chapter 35

Who Me?

And Moses said unto the Lord, O my Lord, I am not eloquent, neither heretofore,
nor since thou have spoken unto thy servant but I am slow of speech, and of a slow tongue.
And the Lord said unto him, Who hath made man's mouth?
Or who maketh the dumb, or deaf, or the seeing, or the blind? Have not I the Lord?
Now therefore go, and I will be with thy mouth, and teach thee what thou shalt say.

Exodus 4:10-12

Who me? Yes, you. This was the essence of the exchange between God and Moses when they met at the burning bush. Moses was a most reluctant leader. He could not see himself as a spokesperson for God, let alone a leader for the Hebrews to follow out of Egypt. Moses thought himself to be a weak speaker with no eloquence. But God reminded Moses that He provides the words that come out of Moses' mouth. Or anyone's mouth. Moses was to offer his obedience and speak the words God put in his mouth. This was all. The Holy Spirit was inside of Moses to work through him to fulfill God's plan. Moses followed the Spirit, and this is how he could speak and lead. The same Holy Spirit is here today to work through us to fulfill God's plans. One of the paramount ways the Holy Spirit works in us is through prayer.

Jesus said the Holy Spirit is with believers to comfort, counsel, and guide. Prayer is a way for the Holy Spirit to move us to be close to God, build up the Church, and fortify God's people. Prayer is to be a familiar act for a believer in Jesus, for it fosters fellowship. When someone approaches prayer and thinks he/she is ill-equipped and unskillful with words to talk to God, then it is good to remember that God gives the words via the Holy Spirit. God listens for the heart in our words, not necessarily the string of words we use. When we read the word of the prophet Isaiah, he drips with fluidly compelling speech, yet in the presence of God's holiness, he uttered, *"Woe is me, I am a man of unclean lips and I live among a people of unclean lips"* (Isaiah 6:5). Isaiah was filled with the same humility of Moses. Humility is a hallmark of Jesus' character, which moves the heart of God to listen to us and respond when we resemble His Son Jesus.

To pray is to talk to God and to listen to God. It is a conversation. When I was in college and studied communications, I was taught that 2/3's of effective communication is listening. To hear clearly, one must listen intently. Often we come to prayer to thank God, make requests of Him, and tell Him what is going on in our lives—good things and challenging things. He wants us to come to Him and talk to Him. He also wants us to be silent so He can speak to us. What He says to you will differ from what He says to me because the faith walks of each person differ. He tells each one of us what He would have us to know. Prayer time builds trust, faith, and intimacy. The deeper we go in our relationship with God through prayer, the more we hear His heart and see His hand moving in our lives and in all of life.

We may think we are like Moses and do not have eloquent words to offer. Or, we may possess a skilled tongue like Isaiah. Either way, God is the one who puts the words in the mouth. But when our words line up with a heart that desires to talk to God and do that which His Spirit guides us to speak and do, we bless God. We glorify Him. We honor Him. What does He do? He blesses us. He smiles and gives us the grace to make us more into the image of His Son Jesus. Our prayers, spoken in the silence of our hearts when we are alone, before family, friends, and even strangers, are times that build faith and bring us closer to God. The next time we wonder about our prayers being heard or performing a task in the Lord's service, we are wise to remember the Holy Spirit is with us to help us. When we say *Who me?* God says, *Yes you.*

Lord God, You reveal to us repeatedly throughout the Bible the importance You place on prayer. Help us, Holy Spirit, to develop a deeper prayer life that will enrich our personal faith walks and foster stronger cohesion among all the saints. May Your heart be blessed and Your plans for our lives be fulfilled as prayers are prayed and answered in the Name of Your Beloved Son, Jesus, our risen and returning Christ, Amen.

Chapter 36

Finish This

I have fought the good fight,
I have finished the race,
I have kept the faith.

2 Timothy 4:7

Abbey D'Agostino of the United States and Nikki Hamblin of New Zealand are two runners who set out to compete at the 2016 Olympic Games in Rio de Janeiro, Brazil. The two athletes tripped over each other in the Women's 500m Round 1. Their stumble cost them athletic wins, but raised them to one of the highest standards of character individuals can hope to achieve, publicly or privately. Rather than continue to race, each woman helped the other to her feet, and they stayed on the track and finished the race together.

When Abbey fell to the ground first and Nikki came over to encourage her, it was reported that Nikki put her hand on Abbey's shoulder and said "Come on, come on, we've got to finish this." That singular act of encouragement and help extended to a fellow athlete (unknown to each other before the race) resulted in the two women receiving the International Fair Play Committee Award. It has only been awarded 17 times in Olympic history.

We fall down. All of us do. We stumble on life's road. It happens to each of us, to all of us. Sometimes there is a hand on our shoulder telling us to keep going and assuring us we are not alone. Sometimes there is help extended to us; sometimes we extend our hand to someone for victory. And what is victory? To continue. No matter what. No matter who. No matter what is on life's road. Including loss.

This summer a beloved friend of our family died. She was a precious woman of ninety years old whose warmth and genuine love for me brings me to tears even as I write this. She died surrounded by her dear family. God gave me the gift of seeing her before her death when she was still lucid and physically comfortable at home. She believed in Jesus as her Saviour, and we spoke of Him and His love during our last visit. I looked at her body weakening and growing smaller, and yet her spirit and her hope were growing stronger.

The Holy Spirit brought to my mind Daniel in the Bible, who was ninety years old when he was put in the lion's den and protected by the hand of God. Daniel had seen many changes in his country over those decades. So did this precious woman. Like Daniel, she held on to her faith in Jesus until it was His time to call her home. She trusted His hand on her shoulder. She endured. She lived out life's joys and disappointments along the way. She was victorious, for she completed her race and kept the faith. She heard the words of reward every believer lives to hear, *Well done, thy good and faithful servant*" (Matthew 25:21).

Grief is one of the most arduous experiences of the human journey. It is replete with unpredictable emotions, unbidden memories that ebb and flow to make us laugh and make us cry. Tears of joy or sorrow signify the presence of love. Whatever a relationship has or has not been, people who depart from this life leave their legacy of witness. When they endure all of life's challenges, their conclusion leaves us the same message of the young Olympian athlete, "Come on, come on, we have to finish this." We still travel with them.

We honor those who die before us by yielding to their hand on our shoulder and accepting their encouragement to finish our race of life. Some days may be tearful and some days lighthearted, but the victory is all the more fulfilling when the path is completed—even with stumbles along the way. Grief comes. It is the price we pay for loving someone. But it is also the most honest ache a heart can know. Jesus came to earth because of His love for you and for me. He died so we might live, not only an earthly life but an Eternal Life. His victory on the Cross at Calvary is the victory for everyone who believes in Jesus and accepts Jesus' sacrifice for sin. I accepted Jesus' sacrifice many years ago. Because I did and because my dear ninety-year-old friend did, I know that there will be a jubilant reunion in Heaven one day. Grief and tears will have their hours and days, but the eternity of no more tears belongs to God and to those who believe in His Son Jesus. This is a living hope and continuous encouragement for those who are still on life's track. We are wise to muster our fortitude and say to each other, "Come on, come on, we have to finish this." May we finish life, finish this race of faith, finish this journey of love. Because of Jesus and His hand on our shoulder, we shall.

Blessed Saviour of all time and place, You give us an enduring spirit and reason to continue. You and Your promises keep us moving forward. Everything You said in the Bible shall be. We take this comfort and courage to heart and continue on life's road, knowing that You are with us every step of the way and every stumble of the way. Thank You, Lord, for Your steady presence. Thank You for the companions You send along our way to help us up and encourage us. We raise our praise to You, precious Redeemer, and know for certain that while this life has its stellar moments, to see You face-to-face and be reunited with loved ones are the sterling rewards that await us in Heaven. Be glorified, Lord, by our continuance. Be blessed by our enduring faith, faith You count unto us as righteousness as You did to Abraham. We continue on as Your faithful runners who purpose to finish our race come what may. All this is prayed in Thy Name Lord Jesus, Amen.

Chapter 37
Conclusion

*Eye has not seen
and ear has not heard
all that God has prepared
for those who love Him.*

Ephesians 3:21

"My Hope is Built On
Nothing Less"

My hope is built on nothing less

Than Jesus blood and
righteousness

I dare not trust the sweetest
frame But solely lean on Jesus'
Name.
On Christ the solid rock I stand,
All other ground is sinking sand,
All other ground is sinking sand

—Edward Mote (1834)

Our purposes change over a lifetime. But the primary goal is the same: *To act justly and to love mercy and to walk humbly with your God* (Micah 6:8). That comes step by step, day by day, year by year. Purposes fulfill themselves. Sometimes we are keenly aware, sometimes not. To reach out for life a day at a time is to encounter changes and experiences of all sorts. There may or may not seem to be purpose in some life events. But a trustworthy God sees to it that it fits meaningfully into the puzzle of our lives.

Tomorrow there will be new transitions to be made—the ones we choose, and the ones that come along unexpectedly. Since God is God, He is unchanging. *For I am the Lord, I change not* (Malachi 3:6). This fact is one that serves to stabilize your life and mine. Our lives do change, but since God does not, that is the foundation on which to build life, and return to time and again when life shifts and there is a need for stability and assurance. Because of God we have it.

The sunrises and sunsets come and go as lives unfold with each one. We are wise to be attentive to time, its value, and its capacity to fulfill purposes for ourselves and for others. We only get a certain amount of days. Since our tomorrows are numbered, we must do our utmost to acquire and apply wisdom, dispatch our talents, and make time meaningful. Often such awareness comes from grief. It registers reality in a way that only the drama of loss can initiate. Sensitivity to our limited time on earth also comes as we age and realize there is more time behind us than there is ahead of us.

Whatever time holds for you, may you rest in the power of Jesus. This embrace is the one that lasts—eternally. May you look ahead, recognizing that the lives we live and legacies we leave may look too common to be treasured, but in Christ they are the highest of worth. To be a witness to God's love and truth, and to leave to others a witness of faith that has been tried and tested, is to leave our best. A life infused with the Holy Spirit's power goes on. Every act—small and great—speaks of trust in Jesus, aiding others in doing the same for their life journey. Grief is often a way that the Lord gets our attention. Hope is the agent that supports us as we endure until we get to our finish line. May we all finish well.

A Special Prayer

As for me, *my hope is built on nothing less than Jesus' blood and righteousness.* Is yours? A book about transitions would not be complete without extending an invitation to make the ultimate transition, that of a soul given to Jesus. With hope in Jesus Christ and a view to eternity, I pray you have assurance that you will live an everlasting life with Jesus. If you have not yet received Him as your Lord and Saviour, you can do so now. To come to Jesus as your Lord and Saviour and receive His forgiveness for your sins is the most important decision you can make. Consider it carefully, but do not let the moment pass you by. Pray the following prayer from your heart. Holy Spirit, please guide this reader and touch this heart as only You can as this prayer is spoken.

Lord Jesus, I believe that You are the Saviour who died for my sins on Calvary's Cross. I come to You now sorry for my sins. I ask You to come into my heart and be my personal Saviour. I need You. I want You. I believe that what You did for me at Calvary was done because You love me. I receive Your love, Jesus. I give you my love and my heart. Thank You, Jesus, for all You did for me to make me free from sin and bring me to Heaven one day. Help me to live my life as You would have me to live it. Thank You, Lord Jesus, for Your gift of salvation to me. Amen.

If you have prayed this prayer and sincerely desire to follow Christ, your soul is secure for the rest of your life in this world and in Heaven with Jesus. *There is a friend who sticks closer than a brother* (Proverbs 18:24). Jesus is that friend to you. You are never alone. Jesus promises, *"I will never leave you nor forsake you"* (Hebrews 13:5). *"I am with you always, even unto the end of the world"* (Matthew 28:20).

For support in your walk of faith:
Billy Graham Evangelical Association - 877-247-2426
1-800-NEED HIM - 800 633-3446

Wherefore see we also are compassed about with so great a cloud of witnesses,
let us lay aside every weight, and the sin which doth so easily beset us,
and let us run with patience the race that is set before us,
looking unto Jesus the author and finisher of our faith;
who for the joy that was set before Him endured the cross, despising the shame,
and is set down at the right hand of the throne of God.

Hebrews 12:1-2

About the Author

Chris Ann Waters is an author, speaker, and artist who focuses her creativity on loss and transition. Chris Ann earned a B.A. from Montclair State University in New Jersey, has completed advanced study in Thanatology at the National Center for Death Education in Boston, and completed advanced study and certification in bereavement facilitation through the American Academy of Bereavement in conjunction with the Association for Death Education and Counseling.

Chris Ann is certified by CLASS and speaks on grief, suicide prevention, and volunteerism. She has served for many years as a Hospice volunteer helping terminally ill patients and their families cope with death and grief. She places special emphasis and fundraising efforts on suicide prevention.

In addition to *Seasons of Goodbye,* her books include *Walking Toward Easter: A Lenten Devotional* and *My Turn to Care: Encouragement for Caregivers of Aging Parents,* in which she is a contributing author.

Prior to her work in the field of grief, Chris Ann had a career in international business in New York City which involved frequent travel.

Chris Ann received a fundraising award for achievements to expand international education programs for graduate and Ph.D. students at the Graduate School of Management at Rutgers University. Chris Ann received the New Jersey Governor's Award for Excellence in Volunteering in the category of Benefiting Youth for her work through Hospice at Camp Lost and Found, a bereavement camp for children challenged by grief.

Order Information

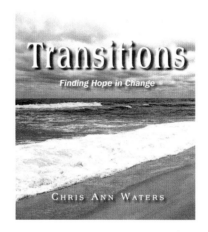

Available on Amazon.com

For autographed copies, contact the author

Chris Ann Waters
info@seasonsoftransition.com
P.O. Box 398, Allenhurst, NJ 07711

For quantity discounts, contact the publisher

Candy Abbott
Fruitbearer Publishing, LLC
www.Fruitbearer.com
P. O. Box 777, Georgetown, DE 19947
302.856.6649 • 302.856.7742 (fax)
info@fruitbearer.com

Made in the USA
Monee, IL
15 May 2021